Cambridge Elements

Elements in Austrian Economics
edited by
Peter Boettke
George Mason University

CLIENTELISM

Aris Trantidis
University of Lincoln

Shaftesbury Road, Cambridge CB2 8EA, United Kingdom

One Liberty Plaza, 20th Floor, New York, NY 10006, USA

477 Williamstown Road, Port Melbourne, VIC 3207, Australia

314–321, 3rd Floor, Plot 3, Splendor Forum, Jasola District Centre, New Delhi – 110025, India

103 Penang Road, #05–06/07, Visioncrest Commercial, Singapore 238467

Cambridge University Press is part of Cambridge University Press & Assessment, a department of the University of Cambridge.

We share the University's mission to contribute to society through the pursuit of education, learning and research at the highest international levels of excellence.

www.cambridge.org
Information on this title: www.cambridge.org/9781009707671
DOI: 10.1017/9781009707626

© Aris Trantidis 2025

This publication is in copyright. Subject to statutory exception and to the provisions of relevant collective licensing agreements, with the exception of the Creative Commons version the link for which is provided below, no reproduction of any part may take place without the written permission of Cambridge University Press & Assessment.

An online version of this work is published at doi.org/10.1017/9781009707626 under a Creative Commons Open Access license CC-BY-NC-ND 4.0 which permits re-use, distribution and reproduction in any medium for non-commercial purposes providing appropriate credit to the original work is given. You may not distribute derivative works without permission. To view a copy of this license, visit https://creativecommons.org/licenses/by-nc-nd/4.0

When citing this work, please include a reference to the DOI 10.1017/9781009707626

First published 2025

A catalogue record for this publication is available from the British Library

ISBN 978-1-009-70767-1 Hardback
ISBN 978-1-009-70766-4 Paperback
ISSN 2399-651X (online)
ISSN 2514-3867 (print)

Cambridge University Press & Assessment has no responsibility for the persistence or accuracy of URLs for external or third-party internet websites referred to in this publication and does not guarantee that any content on such websites is, or will remain, accurate or appropriate.

For EU product safety concerns, contact us at Calle de José Abascal, 56, 1°, 28003 Madrid, Spain, or email eugpsr@cambridge.org

Clientelism

Elements in Austrian Economics

DOI: 10.1017/9781009707626
First published online: October 2025

Aris Trantidis
University of Lincoln
Author for correspondence: Aris Trantidis, Aristrantidis@gmail.com

Abstract: This Element examines clientelism and its impact on democratic institutions and markets, emphasizing that, alongside electoral competition, politics hosts two additional arenas: one where political actors seek campaign resources and active supporters, and another where socioeconomic actors pursue access to state-distributed resources. Clientelism emerges from reciprocal exchanges between these actors. Political parties use clientelism to incentivize collective action and organize campaigns. Playing this "clientelist game," no party can reduce clientelistic practices without risking electoral defeat or internal fragmentation. Clientelism weakens the provision of public goods and skews policymaking to benefit clients over general welfare. Eventually, it generates an economic "tragedy of the commons," as state resources are overexploited and the economy suffers, while formal institutions often fail to constrain it. Even in advanced democracies like the United States, political competition is not only electoral, targeting voters, but structurally clientelist. This title is also available as Open Access on Cambridge Core.

Keywords: clientelism, corruption, lobbying, money in politics, government failure

© Aris Trantidis 2025

ISBNs: 9781009707671 (HB), 9781009707664 (PB), 9781009707626 (OC)
ISSNs: 2399-651X (online), 2514-3867 (print)

Contents

Introduction: Clientelism and Politics ... 1

Part I Clientelism and Politics ... 5

1 Defining Clientelism ... 5

2 The Logic of Clientelist Exchange ... 13

3 Clientelism and the Logic of Political Action ... 19

4 The Political Party as a Clientelist Corporation ... 23

5 Clientelism from the Perspective of Socioeconomic Actors ... 29

6 Organized Client Groups ... 35

7 Concluding Remarks for Part I: Privileges for the Few and Government Externalities for the Many ... 39

Part II Clientelism and Policy ... 42

8 Clientelist Bias in Policymaking ... 42

9 Clientelism as the Inter-party Equilibrium ... 47

10 Clientelism and Economic Institutions ... 52

11 Can We Curb Clientelism? ... 57

12 Can Institutions Curb Clientelism? ... 65

13 Concluding Remarks ... 71

References ... 75

Introduction: Clientelism and Politics

Let's imagine a democratic country, *Politica*. For the citizens of *Politica*, finding employment in the public sector often requires being recommended by a prominent career politician from the ruling party. Professional advancement is secured by connections to politicians and their support network, as exemplified by what a public sector clerk says: "I work in a small town, and I would like to transfer to a bigger city; I approached my local mayor who I voted for, and he told me he would talk to the minister to make it happen." *Politica* also receives foreign aid and administers funds for economic development distributed by a government agency to fund business plans and infrastructure contracts. It is well known that this agency gives most of these grants to business owners who support the government party.

In *Politica*, the leaders of the Labor Union of State Employees negotiate with leading cadres of the political party in government not just about rights applicable to all employees across the country but also for special benefits for its members in exchange for their unwavering political support. During election campaigns, the union's leaders mobilize their members and instruct them to vote for the governing party, promising job security, pay increases, financial benefits, and promotions, as long as the party remains in power. In return, the government ensures that special positions and promotions within the public sector are reserved for those union-affiliated workers recommended by the labor union's leadership and, additionally, that the union leaders themselves are appointed to key positions on the executive boards of state-owned corporations where multi-million-dollar decisions and deals are made.

Meanwhile, ahead of a critical state auction for a major public infrastructure project, the owner of the nation's largest media company launched a campaign in favor of one presidential candidate with weeks of favorable editorials, opinion pieces, and coverage of campaign activities. Ultimately, when his favored candidate was elected President, one of his companies secured the contract and, subsequently, several other contracts by the government. This is not an isolated case. Many politicians in *Politica* fund their campaigns with large money donations by entrepreneurs and, in return, they consistently advocate policies that favor their sponsors.

These are examples of particularistic politics where resources and opportunities are allocated by political actors to selected socioeconomic actors. They constitute cases of clientelism insofar as these benefits are explicitly traded by these political actors for support in the form of political allegiance, campaign money, or votes by the recipients of these benefits (Kitschelt and Wilkinson

2007; Stokes 2007; Trantidis 2015).[1] Clientelist exchanges involve agreements between political actors – the *patrons* – and socioeconomic actors – the *clients* – for the mutual exchange of benefits.

Why Does It Matter?

This book offers a new perspective on clientelism that informs and refines key notions and conceptions in the disciplines of political science, political theory, and economics. Using concepts from the school of Public Choice, a school of political economy that places self-interest in politics center-stage, the book emphasizes *the logic of exchange* that permeates all types of human relations, including interactions involving political and social actors. Political power allocates economic resources and opportunities, and self-interest drives political actors and socioeconomic groups to the competitive fields of politics and the economy, respectively.

Understanding this exchange logic underscores why the book sees clientelism as an integral and inalienable part of politics and the economy, rather than a pathology that can be rooted out with some form of institutional reform. Here, transactional practices emerge at the intersection of politics, society, and the economy. Patron-client relations involve actors who rationally behave like "contracting parties." As the book's sections analyze, clientelism profoundly shapes party politics, campaign strategies, the design of policies, the functioning of markets, and state-society relations.

First, the book emphasizes the profound impact of clientelism on political competition. While most studies see clientelism as a strategy to attract voters directly, the book stresses that clientelism's primary function lies in enabling politicians and parties to amass campaign resources, forge cohesive and motivated supporter networks, and deploy these assets to compete for votes through traditional means such as programmatic promises, attacks on their rivals, image-building, and ideological positioning. In that regard, clientelism acts as a catalyst for inter-party and intra-party competition.

---

[1] It is important not to conflate clientelism with the distribution of material benefits by politicians who expect votes and political support without a clientelist agreement. Banfield's (1958) observed that the Italian Christian Democratic Party had been offering small material benefits, such as packages of pasta, sugar, and clothing, to local voters in the small town of Montegrano just before elections. Banfield interpreted this behavior as emblematic of a broader system of reciprocal obligations. Yet unless there is some form of agreement, any distribution of immediate, tangible benefits, even if they are not driven by ideology or programmatic policy preferences, does not qualify as clientelism. Examples of non-clientelist resource allocation for the purpose of winning votes include any decision that improves living conditions and may attract voters such as building a road or a new hospital in an area.

What is more, the book criticizes normative concepts in economics and political theory regarding the role of government in the economy and society as the mechanism to correct market failures, address externalities, and pursue conceptions of the common good. The book's critique also challenges broader conceptions of politics in which governments are also expected to provide protection from collective risks through regulation and redistribution, tackle inequalities and perceived injustices, and accommodate considerations of public interest, social justice, and fairness.

This book goes as far as refining key tenets in institutional economics on democracy and the provision of public goods that claim that democratic governments tend to be responsive to the concerns of a large majority whose common concern must be the provision of these public goods (Cf. Wittman 1995; Bueno de Mesquita et al. 2003; North, Wallis, and Weingast 2007; Acemoglu and Robinson 2012). Instead, it posits, a focus on formal institutions alone idealizes these processes and underestimates informal practices in the intersection between politics, society, and the economy, where competition exists and extractive preferences abound and prevail, generating negative *government externalities*.

What characterizes both politics and the economy is *competition* and relations of *exchange*. In the economy and society, there is competition for profit and personal advancement in terms of career, income, and personal status. In politics, competition takes place at two levels: at one level, politicians and political parties running for public office, typically through elections, and, importantly, at another level, and before or between elections, competition for attracting campaign resources and a loyal support base without which no politician or party could effectively appeal to the broader electorate.

While democracies have more inclusive political and economic institutions to govern political competition, and while markets drive innovation and the discovery of consumer preferences through economic competition, they both host opportunistic actors who are affected by the very stakes of politics: governments have an unmatched capacity to allocate resources, distribute socioeconomic opportunities, create winners and losers and establish basic norms and rules that govern markets.

Understandably, government power becomes the target of political groups fiercely competing for control over its allocating mechanism, and of competing economic actors that seek to secure a privileged treatment by government. Here, at the intersection of politics with the economy and society, there are strong incentives for socioeconomic actors and political actors to approach one another and reach an agreement on the mutual exchange of benefits: government-distributed resources and opportunities in return for substantial political support.

Clientelist exchanges are thus a rational choice by socioeconomic actors seeking access to special benefits distributed by government and through politics, as well as by political actors seeking to gather active supporters and resources that will enable them to succeed in political competition.

This *logic of exchange* under these competitive terms makes clientelism "the norm" of politics, rather than simply an exceptional pathology in politics; clientelism is a prevalent facet of economic competition in view of the stakes of politics: government's regulatory and distributive functions. Using clientelist exchanges, politicians attract, recruit, and reward key supporters with special interests and specific requests for the government.

Finally, the book explores the system-level consequences of clientelism as it weakens democracy's accountability, raises barriers to entry for new political actors, and distorts the terms of competition in the economy and society, while transferring the costs of this practice to the rest of the citizens and taxpayers in each jurisdiction. In that regard, it ascertains, democracies host and sustain an elite structure whereby the preferences of a few political clients are prioritized over preferences of the public.

Contents of the Book

The book is structured in two parts with each comprising discrete sections/chapters. In the first part, I analyze clientelism as a strategy of political mobilization and a mode of interest accommodation in the context of democratic competition. I explain why clientelism is the most effective method of political mobilization and campaign organization, and why it considerably strengthens the chances of candidates and parties to win elections and political power. I demonstrate how this practice comes to influence not just the terms of electoral competition, but also the properties and purposes of political participation and organization itself, including the formation and cohesion of political parties and the autonomy of civil society organizations and the business community. I then relate clientelism with core concepts in the discipline of economics: rent-seeking, market failure, and negative externalities. Ultimately, clientelism is embedded in state-society relations and profoundly affects both politics and markets.

In the second part, I illustrate how the practice of clientelism affects policy-making and the functioning of political institutions. In what at first glance might seem to be a provocative statement, I offer a simple but illuminating model explaining why politicians and political parties, even those driven by ideology and commitment to public causes, must prioritize promising and delivering special benefits to their core supporters. This game-theoretical argument shows why competing politicians and political organizations in government must avoid policies and legislation that could limit the pool of resources available for clientelist exchange. The *clientelist game*, as I name it, creates a policy bias for prioritizing clientelism at the expense of providing public goods and services.

I then explain how this *clientelist bias* affects the institutions of a democracy; why it is unlikely for clientelism to be contained even by rising political forces and populist leaders promising deep reform, or to be constrained by way of institutional reform. Competition between clientelist political parties and collective action problems regarding party cohesion and mobilization generate strong disincentives against any reform that would restrain the practice of clientelism even during economic crises where economic restructuring and fiscal discipline are deemed necessary.

Part I Clientelism and Politics

1 Defining Clientelism

Clientelism refers to the provision of resources and advantages by political actors – the patrons – to their clients through an agreement in which these benefits are made conditional on the beneficiaries' political support in return (Trantidis 2016a: 6). Patrons can be politicians, political parties and other organized political groups that look for loyal and animated supporters and campaign money. They distribute benefits through political power primarily through government legislation and acts of administration that create favorable rules for, or directly allocate resources to people, groups or businesses explicitly in exchange for their political support.

Clients can be individuals or interest groups, such as professional organizations, businesses, lobbies, religious organizations, non-governmental organizations and labor unions, each asking for tangible benefits in their own circumstances: economic resources or social opportunities granted by government, such as jobs, promotions, insider information, subsidies, favorable legislation, favors with public administration, government contracts, etc. In return, they agree to offer support that ranges from votes to public endorsement, active party membership, and campaign contributions. Patrons choose their clients by assessing the value of their contribution for their political career plans, and reward them insofar as their behavior conforms to the terms of the clientelist agreement. Patrons are expected to meet the demands of their clients, while the clients must remain loyal to the commitments they have made to the patrons.

Contrary to the typical view of the clientelist relationship as an unequal power relation favoring patrons (Eisenstadt and Roniger 1984: 48–49) – a perspective rooted in the study of clientelism in poor, developing, and mostly rural societies (Piattoni 2001a: 9, 2004)[2] – clientelistic relationships exhibit varying power dynamics in various environments. Some clients offer sizeable resources, such as large donations or wide-ranging favorable media coverage, and have a stronger bargaining position over individual politicians and party cadres, even politically appointed ministers (Trantidis 2016b). Depending on power dynamics, patron-client relationships can involve threats and sanctions from either party (Trantidis 2015). These dynamics may change over time. For instance, a political candidate who initially relies on a wealthy client may, once elected, consolidate a position in power, attract new clients, and build a large network of wealthy supporters, to a degree that this first sponsor becomes dependent on the patron's favors, and not the other way around.

In this book, I use the terms clientelism and patronage interchangeably (Scott 1972: 92). Mainwaring defines patronage as "the use or distribution of state resources on a nonmeritocratic basis for political gain" (1999: 177). Weingrod (1968: 379) defines patronage as the way in which party politicians distribute public jobs or special favors in exchange for electoral support. Still, the term "patrons" has been used for all cases where politicians and political parties distribute benefits to several types of beneficiaries (Trantidis 2016a, 2016b).

Clients Offer More than just Votes

Earlier definitions of clientelism see it as a practice primarily deployed to attract voters (Kramon 2019; Ravanilla and Hicken 2023). When clientelism targets voters, political parties and politicians confront the problem of monitoring each individual's voting choice in the polling station (Stokes 2005), possibly with the exception of quite small communities and constituencies (Chubb 1982; Chandra 2004; Magaloni 2006; Medina and Stokes 2007; Hicken and Nathan 2020). By contrast, it is easy to observe the clients' political behavior in the

---

[2] Part of the literature adheres to the archetypical image of clientelism as that of an asymmetrical power relationship between a stronger patron and a weaker client. In this relationship, political parties and politicians monitor their clients, impose their terms, hold them accountable for their behavior instead of citizens holding politicians accountable (Legg 1972; Eisenstadt and Roniger 1980; Stokes 2005). The exchange of benefits between politicians and their constituent has seen as "a dyadic alliance" by Landé (1977: xx), or an "instrumental friendship in which an individual of higher socioeconomic status (patron) uses his own influence and resources to provide protection or benefits, or both, for a person of lower status (client) who, for his part, reciprocates by offering general support and assistance, including personal services, to the patron" (Scott 1972: 92; also Lemarchand 1972: 150; Kaufman 1974, 285; Landé 1977: xx; and Mainwaring 1999: 177). The book has a different position regarding bargaining power (see page 8).

public sphere, especially when they are asked to openly and tangibly support a political campaign.

Selecting clients is difficult for another reason. The benefits to be distributed through clientelism are limited, rivalrous, and excludable, being akin to private or club goods, and as such, they can only be distributed to a select few, meaning that any selection is likely to lead to the exclusion of some others, and comes with the risk of triggering animosities among prospective and existing clients, and reactions from those excluded.[3]

Importantly, the scarcity of opportunities and resources for clientelist distribution means that patrons cannot buy a majority of votes in the population, particularly in larger constituencies. If clientelism were simply about attracting voters, this strategy would have been too costly to pursue. What is more, the marginal utility of a small material benefit in exchange for a vote decreases as incomes rise, making these clientelist offers more appealing only to the very poor and not for those whose "reservation wage" may be higher. Small benefits, such as some little cash or a small gift, are unlikely to sway a voter in favor of a patron, particularly a middle-income voter. This is why vote-buying tends to be limited to deprived constituencies and poorer societies (Cf. Wantchekon 2003).

Scarcity and selection tend to generate a bidding process. Politicians and political parties offer substantial benefits, such as jobs in the public sector and government contracts. It makes sense to select beneficiaries among those who could offer something equally substantial for them, far more than just a vote. Understandably, patrons will choose those prospective clients who are keen to become active and loyal party members, give prominent public endorsements, favorable media coverage and public commentary, or donate substantial campaign money, helping patrons build a visible public presence and appeal to the broader electorate (Trantidis 2014a, 2015, 2016a; Gherghina and Volintiru 2017). For political parties, clientelism helps with the formation of energized and resource-rich political organizations and campaigns.[4]

---

[3] This is a problem that is overlooked by some reductionist models of clientelism. Take, for example, Robinson and Verdier's (2013) model that hinges on the idea that public jobs are selective and targeted, which makes them a politically efficient favor that delivers high loyalty per unit of cost. Nowhere in their article do they model an explicit constraint on the aggregate size of the public workforce or the budget. They focus on relative incentives, not absolute resource scarcity.

[4] Definitions have analytic implications in terms of how we delineate the conceptual boundaries of a term. If clientelism is regarded as a practice targeting voters only, then we can observe its decline with the expansion of democratic suffrage and the bureaucratization of the state or the involvement of elite actors, such as experts, in decision-making. Weitz-Shapiro (2012) posits that clientelism is more likely to persist in environments characterized by high poverty levels, and, when political competition is coupled with low poverty rates, the reliance on clientelistic practices

Clientelism is primarily a strategy of political organization rather than a way to directly attract voters.

Clientelism and Particularistic Politics

Clientelism is a subset of *particularistic politics*, a concept that refers to policymakers prioritizing the interests of groups and constituencies over public issues and concerns that are typically considered claims of common interest. This term includes a wide range of political activities from pork-barrel politics to clientelism and criminal corruption (Della Porta and Vannucci 1999; Trantidis and Tsagkroni 2017).

What distinguishes clientelism from other forms of particularistic politics is the explicitly transactional character of benefit allocations, whereby political actors agree to satisfy specific demands by actors and groups in return for their political support and political loyalty. For allocations of special benefits to be clientelistic, they must involve an agreement between the patron and the client, a *clientelist exchange*, where the criterion of distribution by the patron is "did you (will you) support me?" (Stokes 2007: 605; cf. Piattoni 2001b).

In *pork-barrel politics* the transactional aspect of exchange is missing. The selective allocation of funds to special constituencies occurs without an explicit agreement between the politicians and the beneficiaries. Instead, politicians hope that the "pork" they allocate to a constituency, which is usually some form

---

tends to diminish. This suggests that, as the electorate becomes more competitive and diverse, political parties are incentivized to adopt broader, more universalistic policies rather than relying on targeted benefits for specific voter groups (Weitz-Shapiro 2012). This book has a different view based on a definition thar focuses on exchange of favors beyond just votes. Clientelism exists in advanced economies too, and mostly involves sizeable campaign contributions and favors by organizations or wealthy individuals.

Bureaucratic reform was also said to play a crucial role in the decline of traditional patronage targeting voters. Cruz and Keefer (2015) posit that non-programmatic political parties, which often rely on clientelistic strategies, resist reforms that would limit their patronage powers. When bureaucratic reforms are implemented successfully, they can supposedly reduce the effectiveness of clientelism by promoting merit-based systems and accountability within public institutions. A shift toward meritocracy can weaken the traditional patronage networks that have historically sustained clientelistic practices.

However, if clientelism is understood as a practice that incorporates key actors in the bureaucracy as well as interest groups and other elite networks, as the book suggests, clientelism does not disappear but rather changes forms. Exchange relations involve fewer voters, as happens in poorer societies, but instead occur behind closed doors at the elite level, influencing policymaking in ways that favor those engaged in these exchanges. Thus, rather than declining, the practice of clientelism evolves and adjusts, in places shifting away from mass voter mobilization to elite-level transactions that continue to operate under a clientelistic logic. Studies that focus only on clientelism as voter-targeted patronage fail to capture these transformations that concern advanced economies and consolidated democracies, leading to mistaken claims that clientelism is in decline when, in reality, it persists in a different form.

of government funding and investment, will help them win votes and political supporters from that district.

Clientelism intersects with the term *machine politics*, which refers to the organized efforts of political parties or *machines* to influence electoral outcomes through a mix of clientelist strategies. Machine politics involves a centralized, hierarchical organization that systematically mobilizes voters through the distribution of resources and services in exchange for votes. Unlike the classical view that clientelism diminishes with modernization, machine politics remains a term in use for developed democracies, as these mechanisms adapt to evolving electoral contexts (Gans-More, Mazzuca, and Nichter 2014). However, as noted earlier, clientelism involves clients other than voters, where goods or services are provided conditionally by patrons in search for more consequential forms of political support from donors and other organized groups. Machine politics may host this type of relationship too, but the term has been mostly used to describe a system of party organization for voter mobilization. In other words, machine politics is an arrangement that may utilize clientelism as one of its tools. Clientelism, on the other hand, can exist independently of a well-developed political machine.

Clientelism and Rent Seeking

As a term, clientelism overlaps with, but is conceptually distinct from, *rent seeking*. Rent seeking refers to efforts by individuals or groups to gain economic advantages (or *political rents*) through the manipulation of political or legal processes, rather than through exclusively productive economic activity in a competitive market. In economics, a political rent is *this* specific type of economic gain. Individuals or groups attempt to influence or capture government agencies and legislators with the aim of extracting economic gains that would not have been possible in a competitive market (Stigler 1971; Krueger 1974; Dixit and Londregan 1996). Instead of engaging in production and the exchange of goods and services in competitive markets as envisaged in textbook economics, rent seekers want to gain profits, in excess of what pure market transactions would have given them, through favorable government regulations and distributions such as subsidies, monopoly status, and protectionist measures like trade tariffs and quotas.

Some rent-seeking activities are non-clientelistic, when rent seekers seek to influence regulations and gain public resources without an explicit agreement for reciprocation in the form of political loyalty and support, but instead, through information manipulation, media campaigns, bureaucratic lobbying, or bribing. For example, rent-seekers can mobilize resources to shape public opinion and draw support for issues that will influence lawmakers to take favorable action, often by employing public relations firms or approaching media outlets. They can run or support campaigns that encourage constituents to contact their representatives (grassroots lobbying). They can organize or support events such as demonstrations, marches, or public petitions about specific issues and add pressure on legislators to act. They can recruit social influencers, win endorsements by prominent figures, and support protest movements to simulate public support for their agenda.

Likewise, rent seekers can engage with policymakers, state officials, and politicians in consultation processes, face-to-face meetings, and presentations at conferences or public forums. They can fund research to produce studies aligning with their interests. They can take legal action to challenge existing laws or regulations. They can also exploit existing loopholes to create and preserve barriers to entry for their competitors.[5] Rent seekers can make oligopolistic deals and set up industry cartels to fix prices, output, or other market conditions. They can form alliances with other groups, such as professional associations and labor unions, to present a unified front before policymakers. In those cases, there is no clientelist exchange.

By contrast, clientelistic forms of rent-seeking involve building and maintaining the kind of connections whereby rents are explicitly exchanged for political support and political loyalty, often in the form of campaign money or media support. This typically presupposes some direct contact of politicians through informal meetings and personal communication or campaign contributions to political parties and candidates in exchange for favorable policies, regulations, and decisions. The clientelist type of rent seeking involves *quid pro quo* deals for public endorsements and campaign money (Cf. Denzau and Munger 1986; Grossman and Helpman 1994; Bartels 2008; Bonica 2013; Barber, Canes-Wrone, and Thrower 2017).

Clientelism, Cronyism, State Capture and Corruption

Another related term is *cronyism*, describing the type of mutually beneficial relationships between business leaders and government officials. Haber (2002: xii) defines crony capitalism as "one in which those close to the political authorities who make and enforce policies receive favors that have large

---

[5] Rents can be extracted by corruption such as bribing politicians, which typically involves a more straightforward transaction where an individual or entity offers money or gifts directly to a politician in exchange for favorable treatment or decisions without the requirement to support this politician with campaign-related resources or votes. Bribing for rents can also involve non-political actors such as bureaucrats, judges, and even minor public sector employees, and lacks the political nature of the exchange inherent in clientelism.

economic value." Cronyism is political favoritism through personal relations, which include non-political connections, such as friendship, family relations, whereas clientelism focuses on political support exchanges between politicians and constituents, including organized groups and often involving non-personal attachments.

Rent-seeking, lobbying, and clientelism can lead to *regulatory capture* or even *state capture*. The term *regulatory capture* describes situations in which private actors gain privileged access to, and influence on a department of government or some departments of government, and consistently secure policies and resource distributions that serve their interests. This situation may be the result of clientelist exchange, typically involving wealthy lobbies, businesses, cartels of businesses, or organizations such as labor unions.

Moving to another level, the term *state capture* refers to the situation in which powerful political and economic elites, including special interest groups, exert so much influence over state institutions overall that they effectively make the state work to serve their own interests. This leads to the systematic extraction of state resources for their own benefit (Hellman and Kauffman 2001; Grzymala-Busse 2008). Such a system of state capture can take distinct forms shaped by the strategic decisions of the capturing elites whether to share rents with broader groups of constituents (with mass-scale clientelism) or even whether to allow political competition (Cf. Grzymala-Busse 2008).

Finally, clientelism can broadly be classified as political corruption, in the sense that it is a deviation from normative standards of how politicians are supposed to work in a system of laws and norms, such as a democracy. Clientelist deals, even if they may not break the law, are hidden from public view and scrutiny, and can thus be considered illicit against baseline standards of democratic legitimacy: accountability, publicity, and transparency. Moreover, clientelism can even facilitate unlawful activities. Corrupt politicians can act as brokers of criminal organizations, like the Italian mafia (Cf. Della Porta and Vannucci 1999), and sell protection, while criminal organizations can provide political support, campaign money, and votes. Moreover, tolerance of corruption can serve as a complementary method of accommodating clients who wish to extract money. In Greece, for example, clientelist political parties hired supporters in the public sector who then exploited their positions to extract bribes from citizens and businesses, while their activities were known and tolerated by their superiors (Trantidis 2016a; Trantidis and Tsagkroni 2017).

Clientelism Exists in Every Political System

As a practice, clientelism is remarkably adaptable and enduring across diverse political contexts and economic conditions (Piattoni 2001a; Hicken 2011; Hicken 2020), including emerging and consolidated democracies, developed and less developed economies, and countries undergoing processes of democratic consolidation or democratic backsliding (Kitschelt 2000; Stokes 2005; Stokes, Dunning, and Nazareno 2013; Gans-Morse, Mazzuca, and Nichter 2014; Szwarcberg 2015; Camp 2017; Desai et al. 2020; Trantidis 2022a). Among the advanced economies and consolidated democracies that have received the most scholarly attention are Japan (Cox and Thies 1998) and Italy (Graziano 1973; Chubb 1982; Putnam 1993; Piattoni 2001b; Golden 2003; cf. Shefter 1977). In the United States, the terms machine politics and rent-seeking are mostly employed to describe clientelist practices involving exchanges between political actors on the one hand, and businesses, business lobbies and professional organizations on the other (Denzau and Munger 1986; Grossman and Helpman 1994; Khan and Jomo 2000; Kitschelt 2000; Bartels 2008; Hicken 2011; Bonica 2013; Barber, Canes-Wrone, and Thrower 2017; Schnakenberg and Turner 2021).[6]

It is important to stress that clientelism is prevalent in authoritarian regimes too. Political competition does exist within authoritarian party structures, stemming from career-oriented politicians and the presence of factions competing for support and sponsorship in society and the business community. Likewise, authoritarian regimes need strong allies in society as they cannot survive by relying on coercion alone (Trantidis 2022a). What is distinctive with authoritarianism is that clients can be particularly vulnerable to retribution as they lack robust institutional protections against government action.

Concluding Remarks

From a broader perspective, clientelism, favoritism, cronyism, corruption, and rent seeking demonstrate how the economy and politics are closely entangled (Wagner 2016). Holcombe (2018) describes this broader entanglement as

---

[6] The United States experienced a transition from the machine politics of the 19th century to the special relationships involving donors, lobbyists, legislators, and political parties. With the rise of mass communication networks, political parties and politicians shifted their strategies to campaign finance that enable them to run large-scale campaigns and address big audiences. In this landscape, the nature of clientelism changed from the mass clientelist machines like Tammany Hall in New York City offering services or jobs to immigrants and the working class in exchange for their votes, to politicians cultivating ties with wealthy donors and interest groups through super PACs. In cities, however, like Chicago notoriously under Richard J. Daley, machine politics carried on for much longer.

political capitalism, where political influence in shaping economic outcomes is imbued with relationships in which economic and political elites offer one another mutual benefits, leading to policies that often prioritize the interests of a few over the broader public good.

This chapter has provided a baseline conception of clientelism aiming at avoiding the pitfalls of both conceptual stretching and conceptual narrowing. Conceptual stretching occurs when clientelism is conflated with rent-seeking or pork-barrel politics, and cases where benefits are distributed to selected groups without a commitment to reciprocation involving political support. Equally, conceptual narrowing occurs when a definition refers to clientelism as the exchange of government-allocated resources for votes alone, excluding other forms of support that also underpin clientelistic exchanges, such as political activism, party membership, and campaign money donations. This tends to impose significant conceptual and analytical limitations, as it takes our attention away from exchanges that do not involve votes but, instead, more substantial contributions with greater impact on political competition. Conceptual narrowing has left a theoretical lacuna for the wider kind of actors involved in clientelist relationships, the more diverse range of resources that they exchange beyond votes, and the shifting power dynamics that define clientelist relationships along this variety. Importantly, such an omission would prevent us from exploring the significant system-level consequences of this practice for politics and the economy.

2 The Logic of Clientelist Exchange

The prevalence of particularistic politics in both democratic and authoritarian systems comes as no surprise to those familiar with the school of Public Choice, a theory that started as a branch of economics utilizing economic tools to analyze political processes (McLean 1987; Mueller 2003). Work in the Public Choice tradition was based on the assumption that individuals act as rational utility maximizers, and seeks to understand how voters, politicians, and socio-economic actors, seeking to attain personal goals and improve their own position, interact and influence political decision-making processes and outcomes. As Buchanan emphasized:

> This approach requires only the simple assumption that the same individuals act in both relationships. Political decisions are not handed down from on high by omniscient beings who cannot err. Individuals behave in market interactions, in political-governmental interactions, in cooperative-nongovernmental interactions, and in other arrangements. Closure of the behavioral system, as I am using the term, means only that analysis must be extended to the actions of persons in their several separate capacities. (Buchanan 1972: 12)

Working with this assumption, Public Choice scholars have challenged the typical depiction of government in the discipline of economics as the organization that corrects market failures and supplies public goods (e.g., Tullock 1967; Niskanen 1971; Peltzman 1976; McCormick and Tollison 1981; Haeffele 2018).[7] Instead, in Public Choice models, access to government is competitive because there are multiple preferences and antagonistic interests that are impossible to satisfy simultaneously. Any selection process through elections may generate coalition cycles that are unstable (Arrow 1951; Cf. Riker 1962; Buchanan and Tullock 1962; Mueller 2003). Political coalitions are formed around strong cleavages shaped by group identities, which are fed by, and come to fuel conditions of polarization (Boettke and Thompson 2019). Irreconcilable opinions, distinct social identities, and mutually exclusive interests generate *radical dissonance* that could even prevent agreement on basic constitutional norms (Trantidis 2017; Cf. Trantidis 2022b; Trantidis and Cowen 2024).

Central to Public Choice theory is competition for access to government-distributed resources. Tullock (2005) highlights that government provides an avenue for wealth transfers, often on a coercive basis, which incentivizes lobbying and counter-lobbying. This dynamic creates a negative-sum game in which individuals and groups invest resources either to secure such transfers or to resist them, and this occurs in contexts involving ill-informed voters (Tullock 2005: 9, 31, 51; Tullock 2005: 54). Likewise, competition among politicians is driven by incentives for election to decision-making offices.

In short, Public Choice rebuts the idealized vision of government as a benevolent and often omniscient *Deus ex machina* standing above, intervening with and bringing order to imperfect market and an imperfect society.

The Importance of Behavioral Assumptions

Public Choice theory, like all types of theory, faces a particular challenge: each analytic model and argument highlights specifically modeled behavioral patterns, for example, politicians competing for votes in elections, while the conclusions to be drawn depend on the assumptions about behavioral motives and incentives and the parameters chosen to be included. Take the assumption that politicians want to get re-elected, presuming that electoral competition is the only competition they face, which is determined by voters' preferences. For instance, in Downs's theory, political parties are modeled as unitary vote-maximizing entities that must

---

[7] In that sense, Public Choice theory intersects with the Rational Choice approach, a general methodological framework used in economics, political science, and other social sciences that models behavior and outcomes on the premise that people make decisions by weighing the costs and benefits of different options and selecting the one that maximizes their utility or personal benefit.

respond to voters' preferences. They strategically position themselves to appeal to the median voter, adopting policies that align with the preferences of the largest segment of the electorate. This behavior is rational because it maximizes their chances of winning elections, which is their primary goal, but relies on some assumptions: parties are unitary actors, voters have set preferences along a continuum, and competition takes place in one field: elections.

Introducing observations from real politics as new parameters refines and even tests the external validity of these models. For example, Olson (1965) explains how smaller groups overcome the problem of free-riding to engage in collective action and gain greater influence over government policy compared to larger groups, where incentives for contribution to a collective cause are weaker, and monitoring contributions and punishing free riding is less feasible if not impossible. As a result, interest groups manage to maximize their benefits through lobbying and legislative influence (Stigler 1971).

A key characteristic of Public Choice is an emphasis on incentives in systems of interactions and political behavior shaped by the institutional environment and the opportunities and avenues it offers to strategic actors. As Aligica and Tarko (2016: xiii) note, this can be modeled by theory by illuminating or capturing some significant aspects or a group of evolutions so that we get a better understanding of the nature and scope of a phenomenon in question (Aligica and Tarko 2016: 4). In that regard,

> One way to capture how institutions impact economic performance is to model them as the constraint against which economic actors attempt to realize their desires. As institutions shift the relative price of different behaviors change and economic theory can predict the direction of change in behavior ... In short, individuals will respond rationally to the incentives they face and these incentives are a function of the institutions that are effectively operating in that context. (Boettke, Coyne, and Leeson 2005: 289)

The analysis of clientelism builds on the premise that there is a fundamental *logic of exchange* that governs all types of human interactions, from personal relations to markets and politics. Politics is another field of exchange as governments create winners and losers. This incentivizes political and socioeconomic actors to engage not just in competition with others but also in negotiations including trades of resources and favors.

We can thus look at clientelism as having a supply side and a demand side. On the demand side, there are socioeconomic actors who recognize the state as the main distribution mechanism of social and economic opportunities and benefits, and, therefore, clientelism can serve as the most effective way to promote their interests or even resolve pressing issues that could have been dealt with through formal institutional avenues. Socioeconomic actors want government-distributed benefits, favorable rules, and preferential treatment. Politicians want votes but, more significantly, political allies and support in the form of active endorsements, campaign finance, votes, and activism. These actors are willing to trade their political support for preferential treatment. It comes as no surprise that clients often initiate the relationship rather than being approached (Cf. Auyero 1999; Hilgers 2009). They are drawn by the prospect of selective benefits and, once they become clients, they have specific incentives to support their patron, a politician or a political party. These clients see their contributions as an investment in return for special benefits. Individual clients receive "private" benefits such as jobs (van de Walle 2007; Robinson and Verdier 2013), privileged access to public services like housing, education, or healthcare (Hicken and Simmons 2008), and favorable treatment by the state bureaucracy (Chubb 1982).

On the supply side, as the next chapter highlights, politicians and political parties compete for election to positions of state power, and to do so, they need active supporters and campaign money. Clientelism functions as an essential mechanism for recruiting active and loyal political activists and campaign contributions, thereby creating a campaign infrastructure. Political actors need money donations, political activism, and energized contributions to their campaign, as well as favorable media coverage. They will reach out to those socioeconomic actors who have these resources and are willing to trade them for the benefits which these politicians can offer once they are elected in office and for as long as they have a position of power and influence. Exercises of state power – legislation and budgetary distributions – become "assets for sale," "items in an auction" in a market for campaign money and political support.

It can therefore be said that politics hosts three arenas of competition: among socioeconomic actors, there is competition about who gets privileged treatment by those in power, while among political actors there are two competitive arenas, one for winning votes in elections and one for gathering campaign resources to run for election.

A Clientelist System as an Ecology of Interactions

Clientelism thrives in a system of public administration riddled with excessive red tape, ambiguous regulations, and convoluted processes and, in some cases, bureaucratic processes so time consuming and formalistic that they place severe obstacles and cause long delays to lawful requests. For some, political brokerage can help with securing economic licenses that have been inexplicably delayed or accessing credit from state-controlled banks. For others, it may be relief from tax audits or winning lucrative public sector contracts. For citizens in some societies, political brokerage may even touch personal aspects of their lives, finding a bed in an overcrowded hospital, transferring to a preferred school, or ensuring that military service is completed under more favorable terms. Lyrintzis (1984) described the intersection between clientelism and state bureaucracies as "bureaucratic clientelism." This institutional environment can be the outcome of deliberate design by politicians who would like citizens and firms to find themselves reliant on political intermediaries to navigate the labyrinth of state bureaucracy, resolve certain disputes with public administration, and identify and gain some opportunities for economic gain.

Clientelism is thus a rational behavioral choice, and as such, it is present in all political systems. The practice stems from strategic agency everywhere, and it is not limited to backward political traditions and poorer societies (Keefer 2007; Keefer and Vlaicu 2008), but includes advanced economies and consolidated democratic systems (Weingrod 1968; Scott 1972; Kitschelt and Wilkinson 2007; Trantidis 2016a). It is inextricable trait of politics because of the logic of exchange that permeates all human interactions.

The full range and nature of interactions between political and socioeconomic actors is not easy to observe.[8] For example, when we can try to discern how prominent and widespread clientelism is in each country, we can collect information about the variety of government practices and decisions subject to clientelistic practices. Still, good measurements depend on whether we track and collect information about all facets of the phenomenon, and on how we weigh each of them into a specific metric.

Clientelism manifests in various forms, each characterized by distinct mechanisms of exchange and interaction between patrons and clients. Looking at clientelism as a practice addressing voters alone, for instance, will lose sight of important dimensions of patronage politics. Clientelist exchanges can engulf interest groups already formed as collective action agents, such as professional associations, corporations, unions and lobbies, organized churches, and other interest groups, which would receive *club goods*, special benefits as a whole group, again following some form of agreement for political endorsement and active engagement in a party's campaign. In advanced economies and

---

[8] Clientelism, like political corruption, can be difficult to measure. However, several methods have been used to assess corruption levels across countries, each with its own strengths and weaknesses, and similar methods can be used to measure clientelism, such as perceptions indices or experience-based surveys. See the Clientelist Index, adopted by the World Bank, using data from the Varieties of Democracy (V-Dem) dataset. Of course, what counts as clientelism matters for how these indices and datasets are set up. The book's contribution is to stress that clientelism is not just a practice targeting voters, and consequently indices that focus on voters alone miss out on the most important and consequential dimensions of this phenomenon.

consolidated democracies, clientelism is often administered by party structures and affiliated organizations such as labor unions (Trantidis 2016b), rather than through direct contact between politicians and clients. Large "political machines" engulf party supporters and activists and supporters (Hopkin 2001: 126, 2006: 10; Mueller 2003).

A plausible way to define a political system as clientelist (and an economic system as equally clientelist) is to create a continuous arrangement (Cf. Aligica and Tarko 2015: 119) based on these measurements. Once an inclusive dataset is collected, and a measurement is attached to cases, there emerges a spectrum that ranges from highly clientelist economies where clientelist exchanges play a major role in resource distribution, to those with less political discrimination in policy interference and fewer cases of patronage. We can then define cut points across this continuum to construct categories along this continuum as in "low," "medium," "high," and "very high" (Aligica and Tarko 2015: 119).

Another way to approach clientelism is to identify *varieties* of clientelism, along specific dimensions of the phenomenon driven by observations that support the building of these categorical distinctions (Nichter 2018; Yıldırım and Kitschelt 2020; Higashijima and Washida 2024). This exercise is part of typological theory[9] For example, a typology of clientelism separates vote-buying from relational clientelism or collective clientelism (Pellicer et al. 2020). Vote-buying refers to direct exchanges of goods or services for votes during elections, while relational clientelism emphasizes ongoing relationships where benefits extend beyond electoral cycles and foster loyalty and dependency between patrons and clients in the longer run. Collective clientelism, on the other hand, involves group-based exchanges where benefits are distributed to groups, such as a labor union. Corporate clientelism can be seen as a subset of collective clientelism involving firms and business actors. In short, we can incorporate various manifestations of the phenomenon into theoretically discernible categories (e.g., corporate clientelism versus collective clientelism) separated by conceptual "gaps" between them, namely significant transitions from one type to another (Cf. Aligica and Tarko 2015).[10]

---

[9] In this book, I do not intend to construct a taxonomy or typology of clientelism categorizing this practice into discrete forms with specific characteristics; rather, the objective of this book is to emphasize the interplay between clientelism as an exchange relationship and system-level properties such as the provision of public goods, the dynamics of democratic competition, its implications for prosperity, and the potential avenues for reform.

[10] For a contribution on how to create a robust typological or taxonomical theory to account for historical transitions, see Aligica and Tarko (2015).

Concluding Remarks

This chapter has highlighted the *logic of exchange* that drives political and socioeconomic action to patron-client relations and creates an ecology of clientelist exchanges and ultimately a clientelist system of state-society interactions.

In the following chapters, clientelism will be analyzed as a catalytical force of political competition, which involves competition for campaign resources and competition for votes. While competition for votes is by far more visible, clientelism thrives as a strategy that helps politicians and political parties organize campaigns so that *they* can become visible in the public sphere, and this drastically reconfigures both state-society relations and the workings of the economy.

3 Clientelism and the Logic of Political Action

Why isn't it the case that politicians and political parties do not just use other, more legitimate ways to mobilize political support, such as energizing ideological beliefs and appealing to shared values and ideals? What is special in the way clientelism animates political mobilization and helps with campaign organization, and how does it, consequently, influence electoral outcomes? How does clientelism intersect with the way ideas, party manifestos, and policy proposals become appealing among voters? In this chapter, I will explain why clientelism plays a catalytical role in political competition in the presence of policy goals, ideological beliefs, value systems, and policy preferences, by presenting the problem of political organization and the exchange logic of political action.

The Problem of Political Organization

Political parties prepare manifestos, propagate programmatic messages, and make policy pledges. They represent ideas and ideologies, and they use rhetoric and build narratives to address the groups they want to represent. They criticize their opponents for negative qualities and negative policy records. In all these cases, their success depends on how visible they are in the public sphere, and whether they succeed in presenting a recognizable image or "brand name" (Aldrich 1995; Cox 1997, 1999) so that it will be *these* political actors, and not others, which would represent these ideas, preferences, narratives and ideologies on the left, center and right of the political spectrum. Political actors need active supporters and rely on a campaign infrastructure to publicly present themselves as credible, efficient, genuine, and likable, and visibly criticize their opponents.

The game of electoral competition is *nested* in a competition for campaign resources and effective organization. Politicians and political parties must first attract allies, recruit active and loyal supporters, and gather sizeable campaign donations. Yet here they face an important problem. Campaign donations are costly, and party membership and active participation in a political campaign require people to give quite a lot of energy, substantial time, and at times money, which they could have reserved for other activities and investments. While many citizens can find common ground in terms of political ideology and common values, and may share similar concerns and ideas, they may think that the cost of contributing to a campaign beyond voting or attending some events and rallies is not worth it.

Mancur Olson (1965) describes this as the *problem of collective action*. Incentivizing participation in collective action follows a certain calculation: when a perceived collective benefit will be shared indiscriminately among both contributors and non-contributors, rational individuals would prefer to see others spend money and time to fight for the benefit, which they could also benefit from by just making no contribution to the collective goal or by doing little. This tendency is known as *free riding*.

The problem of collective action emphasizes that having common interests does not suffice for a group to be formed and become active.[11] The same problem plagues political organizations and the organization of political action. It may still be less costly for some, perhaps, to engage in sporadic actions of political support such as attending rallies and giving some donations. But when the nature of political involvement is more demanding, costly, or time-consuming, most citizens may weigh any benefits from making such a contribution against the cost they will incur and against alternative opportunities for spending their time and money.

This type of calculation poses a fundamental challenge for understanding how large political organizations are created, and how they mobilize committed and animated members and gather sizeable campaign resources, as well as how these organizations remain cohesive despite the presence of internal competition, differences of opinion and strategy, nuanced ideological differences, divergent values on other political dimensions, etc. Olson's argument about

---

[11] Buchanan and Tullock noted that:

> ... individuals will tend to make collective decisions by organizing themselves in the smallest coalitions defined as effective by the decision-making rules, and, for members of dominant coalitions, the gains will tend to be shared symmetrically. Larger coalitions than those necessary for decision will not tend to emerge for two reasons. First, a larger-than-necessary individual investment in strategic bargaining will be required. Secondly, a smaller individual share of the gains from collective action will result in the larger-than necessary coalition. If we relax our behavioral assumptions or if we introduce specific uncertainties about individual bargains into the analysis, these results will be modified (1962: 155).

collective organization is that contributions to collective action by rational actors are more likely to occur when these actors expect benefits from engaging in collective action that exceed the costs and, in addition, when the benefit of collective action, if certain, will only accrue to the contributing actors and not to others outside the group, and any free riders from within or outside the group, who did not contribute to its attainment, can be identified and excluded from the benefits that group action has brought about. Small groups tend to meet these two criteria and gain disproportionate influence on policy outcomes thanks to their ability to organize themselves effectively and overcome the free-riding problem.

From the supply side of politics, the problem of collective action becomes a *problem of political organization* that can be summarized as following. Citizens may expect a collective good. This might be a policy or political development consistent with their ideas, values, interests, or ideology. However, as the expected policy and the ensuing benefits are to be enjoyed by many, even concerned citizens may choose to do little or remain inactive if the cost of political action and campaign contributions seem to outweigh the expected individual benefits. Therefore, even if they understand that the election of a politician or a political party to office is likely to advance their goals, ideas, and interests, they may not be willing to become active supporters and give campaign donations with large sums of money. Free-riding applies to political organization too, especially after a certain level of contribution is required.

Ideology can serve as a strong drive for political participation, but, with the exception of the most zealous ideologues and enthusiastic partisans, some, if not most, citizens will still assess the degree and form of their contribution against its cost too, and against other opportunities. They will also assess the capacity of the political organizations they could join and actively support to promote shared goals and values. Ideological preferences and strong beliefs do not preclude free riding. Large groups of citizens who share similar concerns, ideas, and policy goals will tend to remain inactive; *dormant*. "Let others bear the costs and risks," many will say. It follows from this argument that large cohorts of citizens sharing similar concerns, ideas, and values, as well as convergent political preferences and goals, will confront significant obstacles in terms of organizing themselves for collective action.

Clientelism as the Solution to a Collective Action Problem

What is more, even within the same party, politicians represent distinct views and interests; they compete over who will be the party's candidate, who will be elected from the party's list, who will be selected to serve in a public office, etc.

The problem of political organization pertains to how political parties maintain their cohesion and operate as large clusters of individuals with diverse values, competing interests, different ideas on strategy, means, alliances and policy, as well as opportunistic career strategies, all fueling internal clashes, dissent, and the possibility of defections, upheaval and schemes and actions against the party leadership. Party leaders who aim to build a strong organization must find a way to attract and retain a strong and loyal support base.

Clientelism offers a solution to the problem of party organization and cohesion. Antagonistic aspirations, clashing career trajectories, nuanced ideological differences, grievances and disappointments over party policies and tactics are more likely to be tamed and contained within a political party if the benefit that the party cadres and members expect from engaging in such action is to exceed the cost of remaining in a political organization that may disappoint them in terms of ideological line and policy choices, against the alternative options of leaving the party, joining another party, attacking the party leader and risking expulsion or dividing the party, or launching a separate political party.

Insofar as clientelism is well established and offers significant personal benefits to these members and cadres, party loyalty is likely to remain their best option. Devoted, committed, and coordinated party cadres and members will then help the political party to act in unison. Clientelism gives party members a strong reason to actively contribute, align themselves with the party's message and line of action, disseminate the party's messages, participate frequently and enthusiastically in political rallies, and work for the campaign "voluntarily." They are expected to behave as instructed and remain loyal to their leader and organization. Here, clientelism serves as an effective strategy for politicians and political parties to recruit, energize, retain, control, and coordinate party members and active supporters by way of selective and targeted incentives.

Hence, clientelism cannot be seen as a strategy that is distinct from programmatic competition and ideological contestation. Patronage politics merges with these dimensions of political competition and plays a catalytical role in political organization for political parties that want to mobilize on the basis of shared perceptions of interests, ideas, and norms, while helping them to handle and appease antagonistic aspirations, diverse ideas, conflicting values, and opposing policy preferences within their organization.

Concluding Remarks

Understanding politics as competition for votes as well as competition for campaign resources political organization – essentially a two-level game – clarifies why politicians and parties must engage in clientelism in one level while competing on programmatic pledges and ideology on the other, and why clientelism exists in consolidated democratic systems too whose electoral cycles and public debates seem to be primarily defined by programmatic competition (Cf. Yildirim and Kitschelt 2020). To advance their career and causes, political actors must build a support base and run a successful campaign infrastructure, which involves forming alliances with influential social and political actors.

This chapter has presented *the problem of political organization* concerning the capacity of politicians and political parties to compete, which depends on the availability of campaign resources, such as active supporters, prominent endorsements, campaign money, and favorable media coverage. Even charismatic politicians need campaign resources, active supporters, and a form of political organization to become visible in the public sphere. While the relationship is not deterministic, considerable advantages in campaign resources and party organization can influence the chances for electoral success for politicians and political parties (Jacobson 1990; Fouirnaies 2021).

The chapter has also explained *why the solution to the problem of political organization* favors clientelism as the strategy by which a political campaign infrastructure can be built and maintained, especially for large parties that are heterogeneous in terms of ideas and policy preferences. Party leaders use clientelism as a way to unite the party by reconciling differences, synthesizing views, and mitigating any grievances stemming from conflicting interests, aspirations, values, and ideas among their members, supporters, and cadres.

4 The Political Party as a Clientelist Corporation

The logic of political organization explains why party leaders and prominent party cadres prefer to build active networks of clients and create enduring relationships with them (Cf. Weingrod 1968; Roniger and Güneş-Ayata 1994; Kitschelt and Wilkinson 2007; Stokes 2007) These relationships involve repeated interactions with recurrent reciprocation, which helps political parties and politicians secure dedicated, loyal and energized support. Party leaders operate a hierarchical system that coordinates the action of clientelist networks (Kitschelt 2000: 849; Kitschelt and Wilkinson 2007). In many cases, individual clients have minimal direct contact with the leadership, and are connected through a chain of party cadres acting as "brokers" or "bosses" intermediating at different levels in the party hierarchy in national politics, local politics, or occupational organizations and churches (Weingrod 1968; Kitschelt and Wilkinson 2007; Stokes 2007; Kitschelt 2000; Trantidis 2015). Each client builds a record of contributions that serves as the basis for their own eligibility for special advantages.

As a consequence, political parties become "clientelist corporations" in the sense that their core members and supporters, as well as party cadres, see themselves as smaller or bigger shareholders. They obtain a personal stake in the party's success, though with various asymmetries of stakes, access, and influence among them. Their "dividends" and rewards take the form of special benefits or the opportunity to distribute benefits as patrons utilizing the party's clientelist network. This capacity depends on their role in the party, assigned by other members or the party leaders, and on the performance of the political party in the elections.

Party Members as Shareholders

Within the party, clientelism becomes the prominent mode of interest accommodation and a major pathway for the promotion of career aspirations. One's entry into the party and loyalty to the party are not simply a political alliance driven by a convergence of ideas, values, and policy goals, but also, if not primarily, an investment for personal gains through the political party.

Consider those party cadres who have been appointed to top positions in the public sector roles, which is a common form of clientelist favor. They may have distinct ideological perspectives and different policy preferences, and might have otherwise considered staying away from politics, defecting to another party, forming their own party, or even challenging the party leadership. Yet they are happy to enjoy high salaries and the opportunity to cultivate a network of professional connections within the public sector and with the private sector. And they know that their position, with all the opportunities it creates for them and their family both now and in the future, depends on demonstrating loyalty to the party leadership.

Clientelism, by individualizing the provision of benefits to party cadres and members, encourages each of them to work as instructed by the party leader to achieve the common political aims as defined by the party leadership and to set aside some of their collective divisions and value differences.

Here, clientelism defines the nature of partisanship. This relationship binds together disparate personal strategies into an organizationally coherent political body. The leadership can monitor, reward, or punish behavior, deter defections and within-party coups, handle any grievances, and secure the loyalty of the party network with a "carrots and sticks" approach.

Likewise, party cadres, even senior ones and those who are the patrons of other clients within the party network, become, in essence, the party leadership's clients with a stake in the party's success built upon expectations of receiving political favors and other benefits from their affiliation with the party leadership, including the capacity to recruit individual clients for themselves. Inside the political party, these patrons will compete, bid, and bargain for a share of the patronage benefits they could use to build their own personal clientele as individual career politicians.

The Cost of Exit and the Price of Voice

Importantly, the anticipation of future rewards further assuages party cadres and members and supporters who may feel neglected or overlooked even recurrently for a relatively long period of time. Breaking away from a political party on the grounds of political differences, policy grievances, and ideological distinctions would break one's investment in clientelist relationships. Again, cost and benefit calculations govern their behavioral choices. The value of the benefits they receive and expect to receive must be such that it outweighs any value they expect to get from a conflict with, or some form of rupture from, the party leadership on the basis of policy-related concerns and ideological differences.

So, even when party members and cadres have collective goals and policy aspirations, some of which have not fully been addressed by the party leader – perhaps because they are left outside the party manifesto and do not become government policy – it still makes sense for some, if not most of them to remain loyal to the party insofar as they can expect to receive considerable personal benefits as members of the clientelist network now and/or in the future. Rather than representing public differences in terms of preferences, ideas and values, genuinely and assertively, it is rational for them to keep on investing in personal relations and build a personal career, depending on how well they serve the leader and how well they represent the party's line and agenda publicly in their own roles and capacities. Promotion into higher party ranks and securing influential positions depends on one's capacity to perform as expected, deliver favors to other clients, recruit new clients, and mediate between clients and patrons in various positions in the party and the government.

Likewise, dissenters have a strong incentive to stomach any differences and swallow any disappointments regarding policy. If they devote time and energy to support their party campaign, and publicly applaud the leader, they may hope to be noticed and rewarded later even if they are recurrently disappointed with their position and even if they presently disagree with the party's politics, strategies, and trajectory. Where else can they go? They may join another party but their party identity, public profile, policy record perhaps, and ideological profile are a liability that is difficult to shed. Instead, they can be assuaged with promises: "the party appreciates your work . . . don't be angry, be patient, and you will be rewarded soon."

As both the party's leadership and the party cadres have an incentive to preserve party unity despite their differences and antagonisms, this joint interest shapes how party cadres, and political parties in general, articulate criticism and policy differences in public. Party cadres and members will moderate their public expression of dissatisfaction, water down any objection over policy, or even censor themselves to avoid an open confrontation with the party leadership. When personal conflicts arise among party members and groups, the leadership is better positioned to elicit silence or impose compromises.

As a result, clientelist ties tend to weaken the capacity of party members and cadres to articulate an autonomous and dissenting voice; it weakens incentives for within-party democracy and accountability, and dissipates the expression of policy differences in public, hiding many disputes or alternative proposals that could have been of public interest.

A Network of Mutual Assistance

The clientelist network of a political party appears to be rather *stratarchical* in the sense that it is neither purely hierarchical (top-down, centralized control) nor purely decentralized (everyone operates independently). The network is often divided into smaller local and sectoral sub-networks. Clustered into the larger party network, local networks may be given specific tasks and assignments and may operate in different social and professional contexts. In addition, individual clients may see these informal networks as an opportunity for liaising with other actors to gain advantages against outsiders. As this network expands, more are expected to join in, the result of "adaptive expectations" whereby actors tend to make choices reflecting the behavior of others with a mentality that "they are picking the right horse" (Pierson 2004: 24).

Additionally, the political party and its clientelist network work as a system of mutual assistance whereby clients help fellow clients in whatever professional capacity they have. Valuable information is generated and communicated among clients who provide support and favors to one another. For instance, a client can alert someone about a career opportunity, or directly favor a client in a job application or an application for promotion, or offer secret information about investment opportunities, upcoming laws, or administrative acts that are pertinent to their circumstances. Clients will receive priority treatment by other clients, each in their own professional turf, such as help with excessive red tape, priority in medical treatment in a public hospital, speedier processes with permits and licenses, etc. In short, the clientelist network serves as a platform for horizontal connections among clients in key positions in the public administration, state-owned enterprises, labor unions, and even private companies. Within these networks, party members support one another, further reinforcing a culture of mutual aid and the value of becoming a client.

Network Effects

Finally, clientelist networks offer "network effects" and provide growing benefits to political parties and political leaders. For patrons and clients, aligning with a well-established network increases the likelihood of distributing and accessing benefits, respectively, while growing the network's size enhances the chances for the political organization that they belong to of gaining and keeping political power and social influence. This acts as a magnet for aspiring politicians and prospective clients seeking to align themselves with existing, growing, and resilient political networks. And established parties benefit from "clienteles" network effects and attract more participants that join and reinforce this advantage.

Here, for clients, large networks offer something akin to *increasing returns to scale* since their contributions (inputs) provide access to a larger network of political connections and a larger range of possible exchanges. For individual patrons too, larger networks provide greater leverage in mobilizing political support and securing resources from within the network, while their ability to deliver favors becomes more visible and reliable especially as larger networks mean higher chances for them too of gaining and retaining a position of political power.

Likewise, for party leaders, the value of maintaining the network rises with an expanding membership of patrons and clients with increasing returns too as this increases the chance of gaining power, which then attracts more clients who would see a growing clientelist network as a more likely and reliable gateway to political power and the resources it distributes. Attracting more animated clients and larger resources increases their chance of winning elections, which attracts new clients and campaign donors, etc.

By the same token, clientelism raises the cost for the formation of new autonomous political organizations that could challenge the established parties that employ clientelism. This is a barrier to entry for prospective competitors if they remain network outsiders. Trying to build a political organization from scratch to antagonize existing ones seems to be a herculean task. It would require gathering a significant amount of resources but without a network, credible clientelist commitments can hardly be made.

Hence, minor parties and new and independent political entries face a serious competitive disadvantage.

Concluding Remarks

Richard Katz and Peter Mair (1995) identified a model of political party, the *cartel party*, as one that transforms itself from a mass membership organization representing the interests of its members to an organization focused on maintaining its own power within the political system by employing the resources of the state. What is interesting with clientelism is that cartel parties can employ clientelism to become catch-all parties at the same time, by gaining the organizational capacity to mobilize and appeal to large and heterogeneous constituencies, and do so in a coordinated way by the party leadership. As a mode of political organization, clientelism simultaneously serves as the main avenue for interest accommodation.

We can thus analogize the clientelist party to a type of corporation in which party members and cadres understand themselves as shareholders as well as employees whose time and energy for the party is driven by the expectation of material and strategic gains – the dividends of their loyalty and participation. Party leaders, from their perspective, as if they were the CEOs, must distribute rewards and opportunities to retain political loyalty, maintain internal party cohesion, and attract new members so as to expand the party's size and secure its prospects for gaining political power. Instead of prioritizing ideological commitments and long-term goals, members and leaders are concerned with winning power to secure their share of the resources distributed through political power. This dynamic fosters an internal culture of a self-serving organization or that of a co-operative syndicate that sustains itself through clientelism, and shapes policy proposals and conducts itself in government accordingly.

In that sense, the clientelist party epitomizes the prevalence of the exchange logic in politics and government, and becomes a network of clientelist exchanges. Not surprisingly, the transformation of the political party into a clientelist enterprise compels party leaders to continuously expand the range of clientelist benefits they could offer. This has consequences in terms of policy, as the following sections demonstrate in more detail. Clientelist parties employ government-granted benefits, legislation, and institutions for the purpose of political organization and mobilization but also have a strong incentive to expand the available pool of these resources. The tendency is for strengthening the clientelist system. As more government-granted resources become amenable to clientelist exchange, socioeconomic actors have a stronger incentive to approach the clientelist parties and networks for patronage deals to gain these resources, such as business licenses, credit through state-controlled banks, public contracts, and public sector appointments, jobs and promotions in the public sector, favors with navigating red tape, and help with speeding up bureaucratic processes.

5 Clientelism from the Perspective of Socioeconomic Actors

I have stressed that clientelism develops in the interface of two key competitive processes that exhibit mutually reinforcing supply-and-demand dynamics; on the one hand, economic actors and social groups competing for goods and services distributed by the government and, on the other hand, political actors competing for political office. This creates an arena of clientelist exchanges. It has also been noted that government-distributed resources are excludable and rivalrous and political agents distribute them among selected clients based on the value of their expected contribution.

The previous chapters mostly focus on the supply side of clientelism and its implications for political organization and the nature of party affiliation. This chapter focuses on the demand side of clientelism and explores its effect on the behavior of socioeconomic actors outside political parties and their relation to political power. Clientelism from the perspective of socioeconomic actors, including businesses and other organizations, stems from a basic *logic of socioeconomic action*: social and economic actors will grasp any opportunity available to promote their preferences and interests. Politics offers one such turf to seek to secure access to preferential government treatment pertinent to their personal, economic, and social circumstances and aspirations. Alignment with a politician or a political party is a powerful vehicle to promote one's interests, ensure a degree of security for one's status or grasp new opportunities for personal progress or profit, and gain a considerable advantage over one's competitors.

A Wide Range of Benefits

The stakes of politics for socioeconomic actors are high and significant. Governments distribute a vast amount of resources and allocate a wide range of socioeconomic opportunities, such as jobs, appointments to managerial positions, promotions within the civil service, government contracts, subsidies, licenses, and favorable treatment by authorities, generating winners and losers. Politicians and political organizations act as gatekeepers of these opportunities. Private economic actors whose businesses are engaged in one form or another with the government have a strong incentive to approach influential politicians and government officials and, if possible, engage in clientelist deals and develop a patron-client relationship.

Entering a patronage relationship can be an opportunity to gain insider information about incoming government actions through legislation or acts of public administration, and prepare one's plans accordingly. Some business actors, for example, want a government contract and, once they secure it, need to deal with several issues along the way. Political connections and patronage may help others access credit from state-controlled banks. Patrons can direct their clients to privileged tax schemes. Influential patrons in government can even design these schemes to tailor the circumstances of selected clients. Patrons can speed up the delivery of government services, such as tax returns. They can direct government bureaus and agents to promote the products and services of their clients at home or abroad, etc. Private media can get considerable advertising revenue from government agencies and state-owned companies as a reward for a consistent record of favorable publications or broadcasts.

Even privatization, which reduces the size of the state in the economy, offers patrons in government offices opportunities to design the terms of the bidding process to favor specific clients. Schemes of mixed ownership between the state and private actors also provide a platform for recurrent clientelist exchanges. Both the regulation and deregulation of the economy affect the terms of trade and will thus attract a large number of companies to some form of political bargain with political leaders in the government over how these rules will be configured depending on their preferences.

Besides politicians, private actors can reach out to several actors who also act as patrons or operate under the guidance of political patrons: government officials; employees and managers in companies wholly or partially owned by the state may also be active members of the clientelist network "delegated" to facilitate claims by other clients in their own sphere of authority.

In abstract terms, we can say that the decisions of these private actors to approach patrons and enter a clientelist network reflect rational calculations of utility maximization given the set of options and opportunities which they see as relevant to their circumstances and goals. Each will evaluate the anticipated benefit of getting state-provided rents against the required cost of their personal contribution, as well as the cost of exclusion from it and from further opportunities, or even the probability of future sanctions in case they decide to refuse the offer.

Consider an example. A company specializes in the production and installation of solar panels and sustainable energy solutions in a competitive market that is, nonetheless, largely created by government contracts. A high-ranking state official, who has influence over the awarding of government contracts, approaches the company's CEO, through an intermediary, and suggests that while the company's proposal is strong, there are other competing bids that are equally competitive, and hints that a significant donation to the party's campaign budget for the forthcoming election will improve the company's chances of securing the contract. The consequences of not reaching out to patronage are exclusion or even retaliation. Consider another example: a company with a government contract refuses to make a contribution to the ruling party's campaign, and is then investigated for irregularities, with legal procedures that prevent them from bidding for the next round of government contracts. The company has no option but to approach government officials and engage in a clientelist deal with the political party in charge to avoid or mitigate the damage.

The structural context in which private economic activity unfolds matters. This is because any cost-and-benefit calculation also weighs the scope for *exit* to areas of economic activity outside the reach of clientelist incentives. Any economic actor wishing to stay politically neutral for one reason or another, ethical or strategic, will necessarily have to cover any loss from doing so with gains from economic activities in areas outside the reach of clientelist practices. For instance, a large company may consider leaving a market if it finds that local political bosses demand campaign money, if not direct bribes. But this decision will be more difficult if a clientelist deal is promoted from party cadres in positions of a national government, and a refusal to agree on a clientelist exchange means getting blacklisted by the whole clientelist network and the central government too nationwide. This dilemma will be different for a multinational corporation with a wider range of options across many countries to invest worldwide, unless it has already invested in that country or when entering a national market offers access to an opportunity that is very lucrative and/or territorially bound, such as minerals, oil, access to a large and growing market of consumers, monopoly status or a special and unrivalled tax scheme.

Building a Relationship of Trust

It is important to emphasize that the nature of clientelism is such that the expected benefits from entering a clientelist agreement go beyond a single one-off benefit allocation. Clients anticipate regular access to perks and benefits once they become established insiders to the clientelist network and, in time, better positioned to negotiate the granting of more benefits and higher benefits. To do so, they must build a reputation as loyal supporters and must cultivate relations of trust with patrons and other clients.

Because clients anticipate both current and future rewards, and want to avoid exclusion from future benefits, they should also calculate the probability of their political party losing power, if in government, or gaining power in the near future, if in the political opposition. They should also guess the possibility of future punishment for supporting this party by the party's opponent if this opponent gets elected. In some cases, it pays for some clients to cultivate a balanced relationship with all major political contenders, if possible. For instance, some companies or wealthy individuals can give campaign donations to several competing parties and candidates on the basis of the same – usually hidden but explicit – clientelist deal.

Nevertheless, not all people and organizations can play both parties, even defensively. For party activists or for organizations with an ideological agenda, their public profile and goals may be incompatible with the ideological beliefs and ideas of other major political parties. This can be the case of a labor union representing state employees versus a political party run by a President with a relatively libertarian economic agenda, or a conservative religious organization versus a left-wing government run by a leader determined to promote secular values. For some actors, the rational choice is to deepen and entrench their ties within the party and make it more likely to accept and promote their demands within a given window of opportunity, when the party is in government.

Overcoming Uncertainty

A key problem with building and maintaining clientelist relationships is that there is information asymmetry for both patrons and clients about fulfilling each other's commitment at present and in the future. Some prospective clients even face informational uncertainty regarding the actual benefits and costs from developing a clientelist relationship.

A distinctive element of clientelism is its informal nature and the fact that adherence to the terms of the "agreement" by the two parties is neither legally binding nor enforceable in courts. The clientelist exchange depends on some initial expectation of reciprocation by each party to what has been agreed upon and, quite often, on threats of possible retaliation in case the client fails to meet the terms of the agreement. Importantly, socioeconomic actors invest in the building of trust relations with patrons and their client organizations, building reputations as trustworthy clients and looking for patrons who are equally reliable. This, in the absence of formal sanctions, reduces the perceived uncertainty over future benefits and the risk of deal breaking. What is more, all instances, for example, in which patrons rewarded clients for their support as agreed serve as clues to the clients and the rest of the population of the kind of future benefits they will enjoy if they decide to align themselves with the government party and its patrons.

To mitigate this problem, patrons and clients are engaged in a form of *signaling*, which provides clues about likely behavior.[12] One's past and present record demonstrates one's willingness and capacity to fulfil their commitments. Patrons can build their credibility by having a record of providing benefits to clients and, in the event that such record is missing, by persuading that they have a good chance of getting a position to do so. At the same time, some patrons will showcase their connections to more influential parties or state officials, and how much favor they carry with the party leader, Cabinet ministers, and heads of the executive departments.

Probability and Risk Assessments

Long-term relationships between patrons and clients mitigate uncertainty over future behavior but cannot eliminate it. Previous cases of favorable treatment provide useful information for prospective clients about what they can expect as benefits and required commitments in similar circumstances. For instance, a government providing subsidies to businesses known for supporting the ruling party signals the advantages of political alignment while calling for new and visible displays of loyalty in return. Looking at multiple cases, prospective clients can estimate which benefits they can get and how to gain access to the same type of benefits the government has already offered to its current supporters, if they enter a similar agreement and exhibit the type of political behavior. Looking at a range of recent cases conveys information about how competitive it is to get these rewards, who offers them, and what kind of contribution is needed for new clients to join the clientelist network.

On the other side, a client's prior behavior signals how committed and reliable they are and will be in the future. Existing and prospective clients, whether these are voters, businesses, or organizations, can show loyalty through public endorsements, participation in political rallies, or campaign donations. As committed clients they build something like a "clientelist credit score." While at times they may compete with other clients for specific resources and opportunities, they should moderate their antagonisms so as not to be seen as

---

[12] With signaling, one party conveys information to another through observable actions to mitigate problems of limited information, informational asymmetry, or uncertainty related to access to information. This is particularly important when there's asymmetric information, meaning one party has more knowledge than the other. This applies to political behavior too, and political commitments. Signaling also helps reduce the uncertainty that arises from information asymmetry regarding future behavior. By sending signals, the sender of these signals can reveal their intentions or capabilities.

detrimental to the party's cohesion itself. By the same token, previous cases of the political organization sanctioning non-compliance and dissent signal the type and range of *costs* for similar behavior.

From the part of the prospective clients, their calculation of *expected benefits, costs, and risks* is also contingent on how exposed they are to government clientelist practices, which is again revealed by recent cases involving others. Those who want to openly express dissent will have to assess the severity and the frequency of previous cases as indication of the probability that the sanction be imposed in their case; this is a *risk assessment* in which the likelihood of the expected sanction being imposed for dissenting and supporting the opposition is guessed and then weighed against the equally guessed likelihood of gaining benefits from doing so.

In that regard, with their record and behavior, patrons send several messages to several recipients. First, they convey information to existing as well as prospective actors, those socioeconomic actors not yet involved in clientelism, about the range of possible opportunities to gain benefits through clientelist exchange. Their clientelist practice is a reward for clients and an invitation for others too.

Likewise, past and present cases demonstrate the cost of *not taking part* in this practice and the cost of *exclusion*, which could motivate at least some socioeconomic actors to become clients. At the same time, these cases also indicate a range of sanctions and act as warnings about expressing dissent or defect. This also disciplines existing clients. Under certain circumstances, when socioeconomic actors have little scope for exit, clientelist relationships can become quite coercive, and so can the whole clientelist system itself (Trantidis 2014a).

Final Remarks

The micro-level and the macro-level dimensions of clientelism are connected. Individual incentives for economic gain and political gain give rise to clientelist networks fueled by the dynamic of "demand and supply," an intersection of the logic of socioeconomic action and the logic of political action described earlier.

This dynamic has system-level implications succinctly captured by Graziano (1973: 297) and his conception of clientelism as both the "privatization" of politics and the "colonization" of civil society. The political process is "privatized" in the sense that the government turns government-granted resources and benefits into a sort of "private good" exclusively offered to selected beneficiaries in the form of a transaction – a clientelist exchange – instead of providing public goods and services to the general population, as governments are portrayed to behave in economic theory and in public discourse. A perverse form of "privatization" of politics occurs because there is bargaining and agreements around the allocation of selective resources that are excludable and rivalrous such as favorable contracts, subsidies, or regulatory advantages. "Colonization of society" describes a situation in which formerly autonomous social institutions come to be effectively controlled and manipulated by the parties in power, as the next chapter explores.

Finally, this chapter also presents one key reason why political parties in government have an incentive to expand the sphere of economic activities in which favors and resources, goods and services are allocated through clientelist exchange. The larger the reach of clientelism, the smaller the sphere for socioeconomic actors to avoid the attractions and threats of the clientelist party and their patronage operators, and this influences their cost and benefit calculations about whether to engage in, abstain from, renew, or deepen their ties with the patrons in government and the main opposition. This, in turn, can transform clientelist networks into more coercive and controlling structures than what a simple "demand and supply" relationship alludes to.

6 Organized Client Groups

Patrons typically have the power to choose who becomes a client against a larger pool of prospective clients. This tends to sustain an asymmetry of bargaining power in most clientelist relationships at the expense of individual clients or small groups and organizations. Still, this is not always the case because clients vary greatly in terms of what resources they provide and how important they are for the political party or the politicians who receive them. The size of one's contributions greatly determines the bargaining position of the client. A small number of economically powerful "clients" or organized groups may be able to negotiate the terms of the clientelist deal as equal partners. By contrast, individual party members and individual activists in more labor-intensive roles, such as the day-to-day operations and grassroots support of a campaign, have a much weaker bargaining power and almost no ability to influence high-level decisions compared to leaders of organized client groups or very wealthy and generous donors.

Hybrid forms of clientelist association emerge when clientelist relations extend to formally independent organizations such as labor unions and professional groups (La Palombara 1964; Graziano 1973, 2004: 11; Trantidis 2016b). While most typical patron-client relationships tend to favor the patrons, organized client groups enjoy a stronger bargaining position vis-à-vis politicians and political organizations by virtue of their size, organizational capacity, and resources, which they can leverage in negotiations with patrons and their organizations for the granting of "club goods" to their members as a whole.

Consider a labor union. Although a significant portion of its members may be tied to political parties individually, when the union with its leadership becomes part of a clientelist network, this association significantly differs from individual clients who have developed personal ties. In that context, membership in these collective associations allows organized clients to ask their leader to negotiate club benefits as a bloc, while each of them could seek access to individual benefits simultaneously.

Increased Bargaining Position

Client organizations – their leaders and members – maintain a source of bargaining power: they are, after all, an organization that retains formal decision-making autonomy and a discrete infrastructure for collective action. Compared to typical individual clients, these organized clients are relatively empowered. It will be more difficult for the party leadership in government to discard their collective demands altogether and risk their collective support.

Broadly speaking, client organizations share some of the properties of typical rent-seeking groups as portrayed in the general image of interest-group activity, insofar as they have the capacity and distinct preferences to bargain for collective outcomes. Yet, the nature of relations that develops between these groups and their patron political party goes beyond the parameters of both typical clientelist exchanges and the typical pluralist structure of rent-seeking, and exhibits hybrid properties in terms of autonomy and bargaining position relative to the patron party. Informal clientelist relations tend to reduce the degree of autonomy for collective action for the organized group but open a privileged avenue for interest accommodation from within the clientelist network.

In the case of the labor union, for instance, the union members can interact with the patron party not merely in their capacity as individual clients but also as members of a collective entity that has a formal autonomous status and can establish a regular and formal relationship with political power. On one hand, their individual decisions and actions are closely monitored by patrons and shaped by the personal ties that members and leaders have with their political sponsors. On the other hand, organized clients may tap on collective resources to negotiate better terms and maintain some balance in their relationship with patrons as a group.

Inside these organizations clients remain associated with shared preferences for policy concessions and find an existing infrastructure with a degree of organizational autonomy from the party leadership through which they are able to solve the collective action problem with regard to claiming club goods. As organized groups, they can also act in unison to defend club goods for their union.

In some cases, the relationship between patrons and client organizations can become so intertwined that it can be described as symbiotic: so interconnected that a break of this political alliance between these two entities would have seriously negative consequences for both sides. This relationship makes it more difficult for the political patrons in government to reduce the supply of selective benefits to these clients for fear that this would alienate the group, and they would lose their sizeable support of a group that is organized and ready for collective action.

Decreased Autonomy

Still, compared to typical interest groups, the autonomy of these organizations, such as labor unions, is reconfigured by pervasive clientelist ties, and members have a vested interest in the success of their patron party. For example, inside the labor union, some union leaders may pursue their own personal aspiration for a career in central politics and, as such, may be susceptible to co-optation by the party leadership.

Likewise, it is risky for individual clients to defect and break their client ties altogether. Clients have overlapping roles as members of an organized group with separate goals and as recruited supporters of the party itself with personal access to a whole clientelist network outside the union. Clients can develop their own strategies to exploit opportunities in the clientelist network and may place pressure on the group's leaders not to push too far for fear that these ties will be broken. This reduces not only the clients' personal autonomy from the political organization but also the room for maneuver for the group as a whole.

In a peculiar way, clientelist ties can reduce the autonomy of formal organizations to a degree that they may not be able to switch political alliances as easily as autonomous interest groups can in a typical pluralist context, but simultaneously give them a negotiating advantage to promote their claims for special "club goods."

Consequently, any tensions between patrons and the clientelist organization or individual clients must be negotiated with a spirit of compromise. Both patrons and clients would rather handle their differences in a way that will not undermine their fundamental relationship and the cohesion and strength of their respective organizations. Political patrons value these organizations as clients and must avoid making decisions that could harm their relationship with the union. In short, clientelism reconfigures the nature of social contestation and political engagement.

Clientelism pushes these social actors to distance themselves from collective action that would reflect social divisions and constellations of shared ideas and values alone. They would rather opt for opportunistic action as clients based on personal calculations. Clientelism is simultaneously incentivizing individuals and organizations to pursue selective and personalized allocations of resources through patronage as a more effective strategy instead of joining public expressions of dissatisfaction and political opposition. What is more, the party leadership can directly co-opt union leaders when they negotiate over their future career in politics. However, if this relationship becomes tense for a reason, the party leadership can mobilize some of the clients within the union to challenge the union leadership and even replace it with a new and more compliant one. In short, decisions are not formed independently of the clientelist relationship connecting organizations and their members, sharing common objectives and promoting interdependent goals. This leverage can occasionally help political leaders reorganize much of the social sphere along relations of interest interdependency.

In this regard, clientelism can be viewed as a strategy which contains, appeases, and, in some circumstances, could even thwart autonomous collective action through the very acts of distributing individual and collective privileges. It allows political parties to engulf civil society while protecting themselves from the potentially devastating effect of political clashes that tend to stem from within society. Dissent around public issues, social problems, and ideological differences, which is supposed to be a function of a relatively independent civil society in a pluralistic democracy, can be contained. Insofar as social actors become clients, their dissatisfaction can be handled through a "carrots and sticks" effect applicable as possible in each case of clientelist exchange, whereas collective claims are perversely "cartelized" in clientelist networks connecting socioeconomic groups and organizations with political patrons and their networks.

Final Remarks

Actual political systems and economies entail clientelist exchanges between patrons and clients, typical interest-group relations, and a blend of both in hybrid combinations. Importantly, clientelism intersects with other forms of interest intermediation in civil society and creates hybrid forms of interest representation, where both collective and individual action are pursued by leaders and members of these organizations. Social groups and business actors become incorporated into broader clientelist networks (Weingrod 1968;

Roniger and Güneş-Ayata 1994; Kitschelt and Wilkinson 2007; Stokes 2007; Trantidis 2015). This strengthens their bargaining power but weakens their autonomy versus their patrons. Leaders of civil society organizations, such as unions, associations, and the media, can use the clientelist network to negotiate club goods for their organizations or can exploit their positions to bid up for personal favors and further career advancement.

Clientelist networks can extend into nearly every type of institutional, economic, and social organization. This "colonization" of civil society through clientelist ties also applies to journalists and activists, to judges, academics, lawyers, and auditors, and their formal organizations. These actors and their groups are supposed to voice opinions openly and fairly; they are supposed to be able to articulate policy grievances publicly and assertively. Lawyers are expected to represent those harmed by unlawful government decisions. Judges should check political power according to law. Still, some of them may choose to cultivate clientelist ties and claim special benefits for them and their families, which they value more than appropriately performing their tasks and duties. They would trade their degree of autonomy, integrity, and dedication for privilege allocated through patronage.

As clientelism becomes the dominant turf of interest intermediation, this practice consequently dilutes civil society activities by favoring personal and collective strategies to secure special benefits and preferential treatment through clientelist attachment to political actors, parties, or politicians. Yet, whether these relationships are governed by asymmetrical power relations at individual level and at group level depends on the extent to which socioeconomic actors and groups possess enough resources to exchange, or retain options for alternative political alliance or a scope for exit with low cost if they decide to walk away from a clientelist relationship.

7 Concluding Remarks for Part I: Privileges for the Few and Government Externalities for the Many

So far, it has been noted that clientelism is a practice that (a) goes beyond the dyadic relationship between patrons and clients, (b) involves party networks, which are hierarchical and led by party leaders, (c) includes organizations with the capacity for collective action, and (d) involves wealthy individuals with a stronger bargaining position. As different forms of clientelist association permeate formal structures of collective action and policy bargaining, a clientelist system emerges and hosts various forms of engagement and negotiation that combine, in hybrid ways, conventional properties of the patron-client relationship with typical properties of interest-group activity.

Clientelism builds an informal "market" for the exchange of favors. Like any competitive process, the clientelist market has "prices" and "bargains," for the goods and services provided by the government, again determined by the interaction of demand and supply and through exchanges between patrons and clients; on the one hand, demand for forms of preferential allocations and treatment by economic actors and, on the other hand, supply defined by economic resources available for distribution via the state and the permissible scope for favoritism through regulation.

The terms, however, under which clientelist exchange takes place differ substantially from ordinary market transactions. On the supply side there are few political patrons that have control over the distribution of goods and services via the government. At the national level, clientelist supply is generally provided by a few political parties and could be distributed centrally through the government or through its local political operators. At the local level, few elected local politicians can provide or credibly promise to provide government-granted benefits. On the demand side, there are numerous economic and social actors that compete for preferential access to government distribution in an attempt to gain a comparative advantage over their competitors. The greatest benefits are reserved for the socioeconomic actors and groups that can provide sizeable campaign resources and considerable support for the patrons' political campaigns and organization.

It has also been highlighted that the logic of exchange, which permeates all forms of human interaction, is the missing link connecting Olson's problem of collective action that explains group formation with the logic of political organization which, in the book's analysis, explains why politicians and political parties offer clients and client groups a privileged treatment. This also illuminates why some groups are more successful in gaining what they want, while others fail even if they undertake non-clientelist forms of collective action, such as rallies and street protests. Politicians make commitments to clients and client groups for the campaign resources these actors offer them in exchange for policies granting these groups special treatment. These clientelist commitments take precedence over collective claims that have been framed to appeal to the public without being supported by such an exchange.

The clientelist system is thus a system of political privilege for the few, offering advantages to certain groups or individuals by virtue of their exchange relationships with the politically powerful beyond what formal avenues for influence allow for under transparent democratic rules and processes. Organized groups and their members are therefore active participants in a system of favoritism.

Examining clientelism challenges the basic distinction in mainstream economics between private markets for goods and services on the one side, and governments on the other. The typical image in mainstream economics is that businesses in competition with one another produce goods and services to meet the expected demands of consumers. The reality is that, with clientelist exchanges, some businesses play in two competitive fields: private markets of consumers and clientelist markets with politicians through which they gain special privileges such as contracts, subsidies, protections, or even favorable legislation that skews the terms of competition in the private markets in their favor. Here a political market intersects with how the private market works.

Clientelism heavily configures the structure of the economy by changing the terms and conditions of economic competition, and by shaping the decisions and actions of economic actors regarding investment and production. Such government interference in the economy may, on surface, be justified under broad claims such as addressing social needs, externalities, and providing essential public services. In reality, these interventions frequently mask hidden deals between political actors and special interest groups. For example, infrastructure projects, subsidies, or regulatory decisions are framed as serving the public interest but are the result of hidden deals with clients and a turf for patronage appointments.

As clientelism distorts production incentives and investment decisions, it results in either the oversupply or the undersupply of private goods and services in private markets due to regulatory burdens or subsidies, and in the oversupply of some public goods exactly because there are private gains to be made for some clients against other types of public goods. This situation can be described as government failure: a misallocation of resources in the form of the oversupply of certain goods or services that cater to clientelist networks, and the subsequent undersupply of goods – with higher prices – that address consumer needs.

What is more, the clientelist system externalizes its costs. Patrons provide benefits to clients without directly bearing the costs: public funds, contracts, jobs, tariffs, and subsidies are costs paid by taxpayers and consumers. There are also indirect costs that are sooner or later passed on the economy, and on those not participating in clientelist exchanges. Another problem is that these are hidden costs which citizens would have most likely refused to incur had they known their purpose and cost, and that there is no way for ordinary citizens to interfere to change the formal norms and prevent this from happening and/or create a mechanism for compensation for the externalities clientelism produces.

Citizens and taxpayers are essentially the "third" affected parties, excluded from patronage but bearing the financial, economic, and institutional burden of clientelism: the taxes they pay, the public debt that they and future generations will pay, the distortions and hurdles they need to navigate unless they manage to become clients. Quite often, decisions over government policy invoke a public interest as public justification but, in reality, mask clientelist exchanges. Politics, from the perspective of citizens, is a huge market of lemons.

In that regard, clientelist agreements for the distribution of selective benefits via politics can be analogized to private transactions that generate externalities – *government externalities* – namely costs passed on those who do not participate in these deals, occurring against and beyond the formal democratic processes that are supposed to "internalize" the creation of benefits and costs through the political participation of a larger democratic constituency, and its scrutiny during and between elections. These opaque clientelist deals generate costs to be borne by the public, but they fall outside the legitimate process that generates rights that include citizens in government decision-making processes:

> "A government externality is *whatever cost a government decision imposes on us that has not been validated by the rules and processes that make us insiders in decision-making.* Only decisions taken exogenously to this system of rights place us, the citizens, in the position of a third party, and makes their consequences and costs on us an externality" (Trantidis 2024)

Part II Clientelism and Policy

8 Clientelist Bias in Policymaking

Part One of the book approaches politics as a dimension of economic competition, and approaches the economy as a dimension of political competition. It does so by presenting *the logic of exchange.* The logic of exchange stems from the intersection of the logic of socioeconomic action – as socioeconomic actors seek to gain private benefits via any opportunity structure available – and the logic of political action, as political actors search for the best way to organize, mobilize, and control a support base to run for office. This analysis explains how politics and the economy work *in tandem*: regardless of their ideas, not all political movements and ideological groups succeed in terms of organizing a campaign and appealing to the public, and not all socioeconomic actors can gain privileged access to policies and the distribution of government granted resources, unless they gain a good position in a system of clientelist exchanges.

Building on this analysis, Part Two focuses on the effects of clientelism on policymaking and the economic system as a whole, particularly when it is widespread and prevalent, and concludes by presenting how clientelism tends to impact policy decisions even in times of economic crisis, and examining whether there is a scope and sufficient impetus for institutional reforms to constrain it.

Clientelism and Democratic Responsiveness

Understanding clientelism is an important dimension of evaluating democracy's responsiveness to public preferences and citizens' concerns. Responsiveness is a concept that refers to the degree to which a government's policies and actions align with the preferences and demands of its citizens, and depends on the structure of incentives facing politicians and political parties. However, as stated earlier, our projections and conclusions depend on what we include in an analytic model as representations of reality and which behavioral assumptions we make. If we reduce party competition to ideological differences or voters' preferences, or the preferences of the median voter or the collective action of organized groups, we overlook the significant effect of clientelism on politics and policies, and, consequently, on political responsiveness.

Hence, if we merely assume that politicians are primarily motivated by the desire to be re-elected and that bureaucrats aim for career promotion, and if we ignore clientelism as a parallel market for campaign resources and for loyal political support, this understanding can sustain the premise that politicians should be genuinely concerned with the provision of goods and services to the general population so as to increase their chances of winning elections, while state officials will be rewarded for implementing such policy.

Consider the "selectorate" theory that posits that democracies are generally more inclined to provide public goods compared to other forms of government, because those who ultimate select policies – the *selectorate* – is the whole body of citizens, and the winning coalition tends to be a relative majority of that large body (Bueno de Mesquita et al. 2003). Selectorate theory emphasizes the size of those involved in leadership selection, and the winning coalition in this competition (the subset of this selectorate they must win to gain and maintain power), claiming that leaders in systems with small winning coalitions prioritize private goods, while those in larger coalitions focus on public goods. Consequently, democracies are expected to favor the provision of public goods on the grounds that leaders must appeal to a broad winning coalition. Since public goods benefit the majority, if not all citizens, providing these goods helps leaders garner widespread support. By contrast, autocracies that feature smaller winning coalitions allow leaders to focus on offering private benefits to a smaller selectorate.

Likewise, in *The Myth of Democratic Failure*, Wittman (1995) defends democracy by emphasizing the role of competitive elections. Drawing on Public Choice theory, Wittman uses the behavioral assumption of self-interest but argues that the structure of democratic governance, characterized by competition among political actors and accountability to voters, creates an environment where rent-seeking activities are less likely to proliferate or be sustained over time at the expense of voters' preferences. For Wittman, democratic elections function as a mechanism for ensuring better results for everyone by those who govern. Competition for votes incentivizes politicians to focus on searching for and seeking to serve the broader public interest and provide public goods and services that benefit larger constituencies rather than catering exclusively to specific interest groups.

There have been objections to this positive approach of democracy. For example, political actors can exploit the fact that voters possess limited economic and political knowledge and short-term memory biases (Caplan 2007; Somin 2013; Cf. Trantidis and Cowen 2023). They can also exploit voters' behaviors shaped by social identities, group loyalties, and partisan biases rather than mere policy preferences or performance evaluations (Achen and Bartels 2016). As a result, governments can use fiscal policy with short-term horizons and shape the near macroeconomic environment to enhance their re-election prospects regardless of longer-term consequences (Nordhaus 1975; McRae 1977; Tufte 1978).

Still, focusing on elections alone would still support the view that there are strong incentives for politicians to seek to mitigate this problem too by exposing those in government for short-termism and opportunism. Wittman (1995) posits that political competition, analogous to market competition, also incentivizes politicians to educate and inform the electorate, thereby substantially aligning policy outcomes with the public interest, and that most interest groups and political parties function as intermediaries, simplifying complex policy issues and providing cues that help voters make informed choices despite limited individual knowledge.

While such analysis captures strategic behavior and policy options with reference to a specific set of behavioral incentives around competitive elections, the omission to include clientelism misrepresents the dual structure of incentives that guide political behavior. Introducing clientelism and the exchange logic of politics fundamentally challenges the key premises of a theory of democratic policy that only acknowledges one competitive field: that of popular elections. Instead, by adding another field of competition – that of campaign resources and political loyalty – we add another set of incentives for political behavior that highlights why democratic responsiveness is more limited than expected and why government action may not prioritize public good provisions.

Democratic elections and the citizens' freedom of political expression and contestation in a democracy seem to provide the incentive for rational utility-maximizing political actors and decision-makers to show some degree of attention to, and concern for citizens' preferences and opinions (Trantidis and

Cowen 2024; Cowen, Schliesser, and Trantidis 2025). Indeed, politicians want to get elected but, as noted earlier, electoral competition around voters' preferences is only one level of competition out of two. Clientelism introduces a first, and *prior*, level of competition: competition for campaign resources such as activists, party members, favorable media coverage, and campaign contributions. Importantly, the availability and mobilization of these resources shape the terms of competition for votes and the electoral chances of the competing political actors and parties. Without adequate resources, politicians will struggle to compete effectively in the electoral arena. Here we can reapply the logic of the selectorate theory. The analysis of clientelism suggests that, even in democracies, there exists a smaller selectorate – a *preselectorate* – namely a selection of clients and clientelist groups whose specific interests politicians and political parties must prioritize as powerful allies and significant sources of political support and campaign resources.[13]

The Preselectorate

An analysis informed by the study of clientelism keeps the underlying principle that the larger the winning coalition, the greater the incentive for leaders to supply public goods. In systems with smaller winning coalitions, leaders will indeed rely more heavily on private goods to secure loyalty. Yet, with clientelism, we find a smaller winning coalition next to the larger one: the smaller groups of selected clients, who form a *preselectorate*, next to the wider electorate.

Politicians and political parties have strong reasons to make policy pre-commitments to these clients, promising policies that will grant them privileges and special treatment. These are pre-commitments in the sense that they take precedence over broader electoral promises that are communicated to attract votes. Clients closely monitor how patrons treat them. They actively support the patron politician or organization insofar as the patron adheres to their part of the deal. If not, some clients will seek to form new alliances within or outside the

---

[13] Having an undifferentiated approach to rent-seeking would not have helped highlight this distinction between citizens as the "selectorate" and clients as the "preselectorate." Contrary to the idea that the competitive nature of democratic elections discourages politicians from engaging in excessive rent-seeking, on the grounds that they must appeal to a broad electorate to win office, this book argues that the public does not discern the source of these costs that are often the outcome of clientelist deals made behind closed doors, and citizens cannot identify exactly who is responsible for these costs such that they experience these costs as externalities (Trantidis 2024) with a time delay and possibly placing the blame on whoever is in charge at that moment. Wittman's model ignores this presence of two policy selecting groups: Citizens and clients. Ironically, these costs become the essential currency through which politicians and political parties gain the campaign resources necessary to push forward a narrative justifying these actions.

party's network, or withdraw their support or even negotiate entry to a competing network, if possible (Trantidis 2016a: 64–69, 77–95). In essence, the clientelist system creates a feedback loop where groups of clients and organized client groups can influence the design of government policies through their connections to patrons, which involve considerable contributions conditioned on meeting specific expectations.

What is more, political players prioritize their political success, survival, and recovery after electoral defeat and, along a course of a political career, will find it advantageous to cultivate long-standing relations with important political allies and groups through patronage. Clientelism becomes the standard practice for them to survive cycles of election and defeat for the party they belong to. Individual politicians would pay attention and cater for the demands of clients first, because they contribute to their electoral success and their future career within the party too. They are relevant to within-party contests at different levels of competition. In local elections too, clients are the local preselectorates. Finally, party leaders see clients as essential resources to build and rebuild the party's infrastructure for forthcoming elections.

In these circumstances, political parties in positions of authority must enact policies that primarily cater to clientelist demands while avoiding policies that would reduce the flow of resources to their supporters, thereby exhibiting a *clientelist bias*: giving precedence to meeting their commitments to clients. When in office, it is the priority to allocate resources toward private goods that directly reward this crucial group, including significant clients such as donors and organized interest groups (Trantidis 2016a). For instance, in the United States, this relationship defines the interplay between many rent-seekers and politicians (Hacker and Pierson 2010a, 2010b; Powell 2012; Schlozman, Verba, and Brady 2012).

Concluding Remarks

Understanding clientelism changes our perspective regarding which priorities political players in a democratic system are primarily responsive to. Governments enact laws and regulations to govern social and economic interactions, and, in a democracy, this power is supposed to be accountable to citizens. Democracy offers a legitimate and inclusive process by which citizens elect their representatives and hold them accountable through the exercise of civil rights, individually and collectively. In these systems, however, political success depends on sustaining and expanding patronage benefits to ensure electoral support and party cohesion. This tendency becomes evident once we conceptualize clientelism not just as vote-buying but, primarily, as the most effective form of campaign organization and political mobilization – the solution to a collective action problem regarding political organization for electoral competition.

As clientelism becomes an embedded and systemic trait of the democratic system, this relationship of accountability is weakened by the priority political actors grant to satisfying clients, and this generates clientelist bias in public policy, namely the systemic tendency of political actors in a clientelist system to prioritize policies that serve the interests of their clients over broader societal welfare or economic efficiency. Unlike what is expected from a democratic system, the more clientelist a system becomes, the more likely it is for governments to underprovide public goods and privilege smaller groups of clients. The next chapter explains why clientelist bias is the political equilibrium in a competitive party system.

9 Clientelism as the Inter-party Equilibrium

In this book so far, I have repeatedly presented democracy as a political system constituted by two political "markets," one for campaign resources and one for votes. I have stressed that political power grants control over binding regulation and the distribution of government-granted resources, and that this creates competition between actors who want to influence or gain this power – political actors – as well as between actors who want to secure special access to these resources – socioeconomic actors. I have also explained why political parties must recruit individuals and groups who are willing to actively and materially support the party's campaign and help propagate their messages.

Political parties must solve a collective action problem: how to build a large organization, energize support within this organization, and maintain loyalty among its cadres, members, and sympathizers. Although ideology and convergence on programmatic commitments influence choices of political alignment and incentivize action, clientelism, with the special benefits it offers, serves as a powerful personal motive for loyalty and consistent active engagement, particularly when nuanced ideological differences emerge and could escalate to defections and factionalism.

What is more, patronage helps political leaders maintain cohesion and prevent defections from within the party, even when their actions may disappoint a few. The capacity of clientelism to serve as the "glue that binds" a heterogeneous group comes from the incentivizing power of the selective, rivalrous, and excludable benefits it distributes.

This chapter focuses on how clientelism shapes the terms of inter-party competition and the chances of a party to win elections in competition with others. This furthers illustrates why *clientelist bias* is an entrenched pattern of policymaking in a democratic party system, and this chapter explains that clientelism is the *dominant strategy* of each party in what it labels as the *clientelist game* engaging two (or more) political parties.

The clientelist game

Let's hypothesize the terms of competition between two political parties in a clientelist system, the Blue Party and the Red Party, competing for election to government.[14] Their competition can be depicted as a game of two players where, for each party, clientelism plays a significant role in securing party cohesion and energizing political support (Table 1).

Let's assume that the Blue Party is in government. It mobilizes its active support base as a clientelist network. To offset this advantage, the Red party must respond by promising similar or greater rewards to hold or build a similar network. It can do so by starting from the positions it controls in local authorities or civil society organizations that are integrated into its clientelist network. These are limited opportunities at start, but practicing clientelism will still serve as signal of more to come once the Red Party is elected in office. Promises are made and expectations are built. The party base is activated in the campaign period because getting the party elected is the only way they can get what was promised to each of them and gain even more down the road. In response, the Blue Party must follow suit and outperform. It decides to expand the rewards it delivers through clientelism to attract more supporters.

For the Blue Party in government, the larger the number of clients, the less electoral uncertainty it faces relative to an opponent that mobilizes its own clientelist network, and the higher the number of opportunities for clientelism, the less rivalry would emerge within their clientelist network. Likewise, if the Red Party is elected in power, it is expected to deliver on its promises and follow what the previous party did: increase clientelist supply to maintain or gain a competitive edge. And, if the Blue Party loses, it will follow the strategy that the Red Party followed while in opposition: maintaining and rebuilding a clientelist network by renewing expectations and making new promises.

Table 1 shows a game that indicates the substantial incentives for the two competing parties to sustain and expand clientelist supply. Both parties must engage in clientelism to avoid giving the other party a significant advantage in

---

[14] Given the important role that the practice of clientelism plays in campaign organization and with discernible benefits accrued to prospective clients, we can assume that the leaders of both parties and their top cadres have complete information over the payoffs from available choices: Not only to engage in or not engage in clientelism, but also to expand or reduce clientelism.

Table 1 The clientelist options and pay-offs for two major political parties

		Blue Party	
		Engage and expand	**Reduce or abstain**
Red Party	Engage and expand	Both parties maintain a strong mobilization capacity, and can retain cohesion	The Red Party has an advantage in political campaign mobilization
	Reduce or abstain	The Blue Party has an advantage in political campaign mobilization	Both parties have weaker mobilization capacity, weaker cohesion, and are exposed to competition by third parties

gathering campaign resources for mobilizing voters. Each party, while in an elected office, has an incentive to increase the range and reach of clientelist supply to build a larger and more energized base of supporters. The other party must offset any lost ground by following suit, delivering patronage benefits in the offices it controls or making pledges for more patronage when elected in office. In this game, a unilateral move by one political party to reduce the scope and intensity of the patronage it offers would grant their opponent party a competitive advantage in political organization and, ultimately, electoral mobilization. This dynamic reinforces the clientelist system, as both parties become increasingly invested in clientelist practices to secure and retain power. Their prime focus remains on rewarding loyal supporters rather than addressing broader policy goals or public needs. Clientelism emerges as the dominant strategy and the political parties are trapped in a Nash equilibrium.

Looking at the clientelist game, we can discern that the dynamic is akin to an arms race, where each party feels compelled to match or surpass the clientelist benefits provided by the other. This clientelist arms race has significant political and policy-related consequences. The more the practice of clientelism becomes rooted and expanded, the more difficult it becomes for a party in government to reduce or withdraw its clientelist commitments without risking a substantial loss of support, loyalty, and cohesion. By contrast, the most likely outcome of this situation is a cycle of escalating clientelist commitments where each party's efforts to outdo the other intensifies the practice. The supply of clientelism grows.

Responding to arguments that democratic competition incentivizes politicians to produce policies that favor the provision of public goods or at least meet the demands of larger groups of voters, this model shows why political parties shift the focus from public goods to providing special benefits to their clientele, rather than pursuing broad, welfare-enhancing policies, and why this is the rational strategy for electoral success. Here, the clientelist game points out that models of inter-party competition that only assume competition for votes, for instance Down's economic theory of democracy (1957), omit to capture an important dimension of political reality regarding political strategy and subsequently choices over policymaking.

The clientelist game indicates why, even if this practice grows to strain public resources and heavily distort economic activity, there are strong incentives for the two parties to continue to channel substantial funds into clientelist benefits to groups of key supporters. The political party in government cannot reduce the supply of rents and benefits to clients and client organized groups without risking alienating key supporters, triggering defections, and causing internal discontent within these groups, which can lead to a loss of clients and ultimately undermine the party's control over the organization with losses in the strength and visibility of its political campaign (Trantidis 2016a).

The terms of the clientelist game do not rule out situations in which politicians and political parties face dilemmas on how to provide public goods that would benefit everyone while pleasing specific groups (Munshi 2022). Elections still put pressure on political parties in government and politicians to talk about general policies that would benefit the many. However, the incentives from clientelism are such that the provision of public goods become a residual consideration; these considerations can be thought of and materialize into action after politicians and parties have secured a loyal and animated support base, otherwise they would not be in a position to make any credible commitments for public policy in the first place or even remain visible in the electoral campaign anyway. Fortunately for them, some policies providing public goods allow for government contracts and legislation that could be fashioned to favor specific clients. Alternatively, governments can borrow or tax even more in order to deliver a substantial number of public services while simultaneously catering for a growing political clientele.

Concluding Remarks

If we acknowledge that clientelism is an indispensable mode of political organization and campaigning in elections, the assumption that governments will prioritize the provision of public goods, and the overall economic and social welfare ignores the dynamics of collective action and the nature of political competition as dependent on the distribution of campaign resources among competing parties and politicians. A realistic representation of democratic politics under clientelism reveals a system of transactional, discriminatory, and elite-oriented policymaking, which is a significant departure from democratic ideals and public expectations.

The clientelist game can be seen as a downward spiral that is fueled by rational strategies for political and socioeconomic actors, which are trapped in a Nash equilibrium in a multi-party system. As the next chapters highlight, there are strong incentives to maintain and expand the practice of clientelism in ways that alter economic policies and economic institutions, there are weak incentives for universalist allocations and clearly defined rules of the game, this further hampers the development of autonomous civil society organizations that can resist and contest this system, and there are weak incentives to pursue reforms to reverse course. What this chapter shows here as a *political* vicious circle becomes an *economic* vicious circle that, once unleashed, can hardly be arrested and reversed despite its devastating effects on society and the economy. Clientelism becomes a self-reinforcing practice even in deteriorating economic and fiscal conditions.

At this point, it is important to pause and consider that just looking at the formal rules of the political game does not give us an accurate picture of the actions, relations, and decisions that have consequences on politics and the economy. Formal rules, as will be noted further below, do not suffice to constrain opportunistic behavior and do not prevent unequal access to power when this inequality is the result of possessing government power and using it as a currency for personal gain, or possessing resources that you can trade for privileged access to policymaking, secretively out of the public eye. Political competition and access to government may be circumscribed by formal rules and institutions but these formal rules are permeable to informal relationships and interpersonal connections.

Likewise, whichever visions of politics one holds as conducive to general welfare-maximizing outcomes, whether from the right or the left, from social democracy to neoliberalism, from monetarism to Keynesianism, etc., a discussion on expected outcomes, repercussions, and side effects must include a consideration of clientelist relations and its system-level consequences, which the next chapter explores.

The reality is that democratic politics are defined by incentives that favor and sustain the creation of privilege for political insiders, which stands in stark contrast to core ideals of democracy that emphasize representation, public accountability, deliberation, responsiveness, and fair competition for the votes of citizens. And, in that sense, while political theory may dismiss clientelism as a pathology of politics, clientelism itself is part and parcel of the physiology of politics. This is what politics is.

10 Clientelism and Economic Institutions

The prosperity of advanced economies has been associated with the quality of their institutions and how they structure competitive market forces to produce goods and services while constraining rent-seeking (Buchanan and Brennan 1985; Buchanan 2000). By contrast, poor economic performance is associated with the decline of these institutions and the degree to which political power can manipulate markets to the advantage of few vested interests. North, Wallis, and Weingast (2007; Also, North, Wallis, and Weingast 2009) differentiate between "limited access orders," where a small elite controls resources and power granting privileges to a few, and "open access orders," where access to resources and political power is more widely available thanks to established institutions preserving market mechanisms of wealth creation, such as property rights, legal frameworks, and financial systems. When political power is decentralized or constrained by institutions, this reduces the likelihood of elite capture and monopolization (Van Bavel 2016).

This chapter explains how clientelism becomes the pathway through which even advanced economies can transition to systems with reserved privileges for few insiders. Building on the clientelist game, I show how clientelism can unleash a vicious cycle for the economy, in which governments choose fiscally profligate policies and raise barriers to entrepreneurship in order to sustain their clientelist practices. This leads to poor economic performance, which in turn further fuels the demand for clientelism by those seeking protection and favoritism, which then distorts the economy, etc. Over time, this pattern leads to soaring fiscal deficits, high levels of national debt, and, eventually, an economic crisis as the economy cannot sustain government spending and the state's capacity to finance its obligations diminishes. Lamentably, as this chapter shows, the erosion of relatively open access systems is easier and more likely to happen than an effort to move a country from conditions of a limited access system to a more open access system.

A vicious circle

The demand for clientelism tends to grow. As social actors observe others gaining access to state-distributed resources through clientelist exchanges, they seek similar arrangements, especially if their competitors are already benefiting from them. Political actors, particularly those in power, face increasing pressures to satisfy the growing demand for patronage. They must respond by offering more patronage, which inadvertently invites even greater demands from current and prospective clients. To sustain this cycle, they must increase government spending or redirect state functions, public policies, and institutions into the turf of clientelist exchange. Consequently, more economic actors become reliant on government allocations, and tied to patron-client affiliations and political loyalty. Growing demand fuels an increase in supply.

This supply-and-demand dynamic pushes the economy further away from the principles of an open-access system, ideally a type of economy characterized by minimal barriers to entry, transparent rules and secure property rights, and takes it closer to a structure skewed to benefit political insiders. In such a system, success, or even survival, becomes contingent on access to patronage networks.

The growth of clientelism also undermines the autonomy of civil society, which is supposed to serve as a check on political power and a pillar of a pluralist society. Citizens and their organizations rely heavily on political parties and patron-client networks to secure access to resources and promote their goals. Greater dependency on party patronage stifles the emergence of a relatively independent civil society capable of checking political power. This demoralizes citizens who expect civil society to genuinely voice their concerns, and democratic politics to yield better societal and economic outcomes collectively. Many become cynical or apathetic, seeing little reason to vote or engage politically. Similarly, pervasive clientelism discourages individuals who once aspired to enter politics to serve the public or advocate for ideas. Only the patrons get "on top." These politicians, facing little friction from a largely co-opted or apathetic civil society, further engage in corruption and clientelist practices (Manzetti and Wilson 2007; Trantidis and Tsagkroni 2017).

Without internal political or societal resistance, more resources are diverted to sustain patronage networks, leaving less for essential public goods like infrastructure, education, and healthcare. In the end, the dynamic of clientelism is such that it prevails over any source of pressure from within politics, the business community, and civil society pushing for breaks on clientelism and for reforms for better economic performance.

Economic crisis

Growing clientelism sacrifices long-term economic growth and fiscal stability leading to poor economic performance. Over time, excessive government spending and borrowing to sustain clientelist practices undermine private investment and divert funds to government-backed projects that primarily benefit client businesses. Furthermore, protectionism and unfair competition render some industries globally uncompetitive, deterring foreign investment due to regulatory uncertainty and high costs. These effects exacerbate income inequality, lower living standards, and result in the under-provision of public goods, leaving society to bear the long-term costs. The growth of clientelism leads to a situation where the country's economic dynamism is exhausted and the country faces deteriorating economic and fiscal conditions (Krueger 1974; Trantidis 2016a; Cf. Tullock 1967). The economy experiences stagnation, declining public services, increasing public dissatisfaction, and, ultimately, an economic crisis.

This crisis can be understood through the metaphor of "the tragedy of the commons." The tragedy of the commons occurs when individuals, acting in their own self-interest, overuse and deplete shared resources, ultimately to the detriment of the entire community. In the short term, they seem to be acting rationally, seeking to maximize their share of the benefits, but show no regard to the long-term consequences because no single actor bears the full cost of their exploitation. A classic example of the tragedy of the commons is a shared pasture used by multiple herdsmen, where each herdsman, acting in their self-interest, adds more animals to graze than the pasture can sustainably support. As a result, the collective overgrazing leads to the degradation of the pasture, eventually harming all users as it becomes barren and unable to sustain any livestock.

With clientelism, the "commons" represents the state's resources and fiscal capacity and, ultimately, the economy and its prospects. The analogy with the case of clientelism involves political parties and politicians as the "herdsmen," and clients and organizations as the "grazing sheep," while public resources and economic activities are "common pasture" that is exploited by those rushing to benefit from patronage before someone else steals their share. If some players refuse to play the clientelist game, their competitors will gain an advantage over them. Unfortunately, as noted earlier, engaging in clientelism remains the dominant strategy for political contestants. This constrains the room of maneuver for both the government and the party in opposition to introduce limits to this practice. Opportunism unravels "as if there is no tomorrow."

By the time the effects are fully felt by the population, the damage is already done. At this point, under dire economic circumstances, there may be no sufficient financial room for policies that cater for larger constituencies, such as welfare spending, public infrastructure building, lowering taxes, or supporting lower incomes. Still, political parties and politicians know that sticking with clientelism can save them from total political demise. The campaign resources that this practice gives them, such as supporters and campaign money, are vital for their survival and, after all, they can use these resources to push their own preferred narrative over the causes of the crisis while simultaneously putting the blame on their political opponents or on other actors, groups and institutions, national or international, targeted as scapegoats.

For some countries, the writing was on the wall. In Greece, for decades, the two main political parties, *New Democracy* from the center-right and *PASOK* from the center-left, developed large clientelist networks that comprised labor unions, professional organizations, and business actors. The terms of their competition were such that leaders of both parties understood that if one of them had refrained from satisfying the party's political clientele, this would have weakened its own political cohesion and electoral campaign, leaving the opposition party in a stronger position to attract supporters by promising to restore or even expand clientelist benefits. This competition for clientelist supply led to excessive public spending, unsustainable borrowing, and weak enforcement of tax collection, ultimately plunging the economy into crisis and fiscal collapse (Trantidis 2016a).

Venezuela, under the leadership of Hugo Chávez and his successor Nicolás Maduro, provides another extreme example of clientelism, corruption, and mismanagement leading to economic disaster. The Venezuelan government used state oil revenues to fund extensive social programs and subsidies deployed to secure political loyalty with direct cash transfers and public sector employment for supporters. When global oil prices fell in the mid-2010s, the Venezuelan economy was exposed as highly vulnerable. Even as the economy disintegrated with hyperinflation, severe shortages of basic goods, and a humanitarian crisis, the Maduro government maintained its clientelist practices to secure loyalty from the military and other key groups, and to fend off support for the political opposition, leading to the near-total collapse of a resource-rich country. The Venezuelan case exemplifies why clientelism remains the best strategy for a single dominant party in the government to follow in order to cling to power while running a country in crisis.

In other advanced democracies, clientelism and rent-seeking coexist with relatively good economic performance insofar as efficient sectors of the economy remain robust and outward-looking, and the economy and public finances are not overwhelmed by the costs and inefficiencies of clientelist practices (Khan and Jomo 2000; Hicken 2011; Kitschelt 2007). South Korea, Singapore, and Taiwan are such cases, where big corporations are benefiting from patronage ties with the government, but the government also opts for policies designed to make them globally competitive.

In most cases, however, clientelism contributes to poverty and economic inequality (Nichter 2010; Stokes 2021) in sub-Saharan Africa, Latin America, the Middle East, Central Asia, and Eastern Europe. Embedded patterns of elite predation and clientelism rest upon weak institutions and unequal treatment that contribute to economic stagnation and the exploitation of society by a few insiders. What is worse, clientelist systems fuel political polarization and, particularly in poorer societies, fierce confrontation and conflict as the stakes of politics are high and living conditions remain poor for the many, further contributing to political conflict, rampant short-termism and opportunism, declining social conditions, and economic malaise.

Importantly, looking at clientelism as a vicious circle raises the alarm on the direction of advanced economies such as the US, where we can also observe powerful special interest groups lobbying the policymaking process (Grossman and Helpman 1994, 2001; Brady, Verba, and Schlozman 1995; Kroszner and Stratmann 2005; Lindsey and Teles 2017; Winter and Page 2009) and, most probably, engaging in clientelist exchanges with politicians behind closed doors to influence policy in exchange for financial contributions to campaigns and other forms of political support (Gilens and Page 2014). This process indicates a *quid pro* quo logic and triggers a similar downward spiral whereby the stakes of politics are getting heightened, fueling corruption, clientelism, and polarization.

Concluding Remarks

Olson (2000) distinguishes how different types of governance impact economic performance and societal well-being. He argues that "stationary bandits," who become established rulers of a territory, develop a vested interest in its long-term prosperity and are more likely to foster stable and sustainable governance. In contrast, "roving bandits" exploit resources for immediate gains without concern for future consequences. Olson (2000) argues that societies fall apart when there is a stronger incentive for their members to extract rather than to create, when there is greater gain from predation than from productive and mutually beneficial activities.

This chapter illustrates how the clientelist game creates the type of race where political parties and politicians alternating in power use their time and energy while in office to expand their clientelist ties and exploit as many resources as possible. In this sense, they behave like the "roving bandits" described by Olson (2000). Extractive elected governments tend to have shorter political life cycles. This generates a situation that can be described as the "tragedy of the commons," an analogy that illustrates two key risks: the tendency of clientelism to expand in any political system and the systemic and inescapable damage that this practice does to the economy.

Democracies have mechanisms to mitigate the tendency for alternating extraction, provided there is an institutional framework that ensures power is shared, state power is exercised under clear rules and judicial oversight, and no political or social group can fully dominate public authority, while alternation in public offices occurs regularly under the scrutiny of an active, vigilant and relatively independent and pluralist civil society. Checks on extractive tendencies can be embedded at the constitutional level too.

However, the significance of institutions in limiting state capture should not be overstated. For institutions to function effectively, there must also be informal checks and balances from within society – namely, the capacity of groups to oppose political extraction. Yet this capacity is often constrained by collective action problems and, as subsequent sections will show, by the pervasive influence of clientelism itself on the formal system of checks and balances.

Clientelism, as noted earlier, is a powerful set of incentives and disincentives for participation in public life. It engulfs and co-opts politics, society, and the economy. And without strong and relatively independent civil society pushing for transparency, fairness, and accountability, political elites face little resistance in their plans to intensify the clientelist system. Clientelism unleashes an almost unbreakable vicious political cycle and an ensuing vicious economic circle, leading to dual and chronic, institutional and economic decline.

11 Can We Curb Clientelism?

Consider an optimistic scenario: Amidst widespread public frustration with economic stagnation, corruption, falling living standards, and rising uncertainty, a leader of a political party comes as a disruptive force in the political landscape and gains popularity. Positioning himself as an outsider, he capitalizes on public dissatisfaction with the practices of clientelism by the established parties whose popularity is now on free fall. His campaign chastises patronage networks and attacks the establishment with a populist message that resonates with the public. Using sensational rhetoric and thriving on social media, he pledges to make the economy work for everyone. He vows to "clean up politics," root out corruption, dismantle clientelist networks, and "drain the swamp." He projects an explicit rejection of the status quo.

Another scenario involves a government deeply entrenched in a clientelist system confronting the pressures of an imminent economic crisis. Faced with rising fiscal costs and economic underperformance caused by years of patronage politics, the government comes to a point where it feels compelled to change course in its economic policy and even reform key economic institutions to stabilize and revamp the economy. Public discontent over declining living standards and economic stagnation has intensified. The public opinion is restless.

During an economic crisis, the government faces a political dilemma, "to reform or not to reform." A crisis opens the possibility for more radical institutional reform with profound changes in the embedded incentives and norms guiding collective behavior in the system. When economic conditions seriously worsen, and patronage politics generate a heavy burden on the economy and the stability of the political system itself, these conditions become a political liability for the party in government. There will be pressure from the people themselves as well as from market investors for substantial reform to make governance more transparent and efficient, cut down government spending, balance the budget, and boost the competitiveness of the economy. Under these circumstances, even political forces reliant on clientelism might consider pursuing a reform agenda. This could include measures like fiscal consolidation and structural reforms aimed at curbing the excesses of clientelism. Economic reform seems inevitable to prevent an economic crisis and fiscal collapse, and the government usually finds some room for maneuver to implement such reforms (Evans 1992; Waterbury 1992; Geddes 1994).

Is an economic crisis, and often the advent of a political outsider in those extraordinary circumstances, a window of opportunity for the system to be reformed in ways that will limit the opportunities for clientelist exchange in the years to come?

Cycles of Crisis and Reform: The Case of Argentina

Let's consider the first scenario of a political outsider disrupting the clientelist system. At the time I was writing this book, President Javier Milei of Argentina had embarked on a controversial reform agenda of fiscal consolidation and deregulation, driven by his fervent ideological commitment to economic liberalism. Milei's rhetoric and policy agenda raises an important question. Are political outsiders, those political leaders not yet embedded in the clientelist game described above, capable of taming the practice of clientelism?

Milei positions himself as a disruptor of Argentina's deeply entrenched clientelist system. He has garnered significant support from segments of the middle class and business community, including prominent business leaders and some media outlets, that oppose the Peronist party that was previously in government. Such support may compensate for the lack of a mass clientelist base and resourceful clients. In the meantime, Milei has relied on populist rhetoric to offset the Peronist narrative, targeting voters, especially from the middle classes, who were feeling enraged with Argentina's condition of almost permanent economic crisis.[15] His libertarian ideology has emphasized promoting a smaller state and a free-market economy, and has been coupled with a populist narrative that blames groups associated with, or tainted with accusations of clientelism and corruption for Argentina's crisis. His declared vision has included liberalizing the economy, reducing state intervention, encouraging private investment, and stabilizing Argentina's macroeconomic environment.

Milei is not the first President of Argentina to have promised deep reforms or to have actually implemented reforms. Carlos Menem (1989–1999), Fernando de la Rúa (1999–2001), and Mauricio Macri (2015–2019) were also elected with a similar commitment to reform the economy, and implemented policies of structural reform that did not, however, dismantle deep-rooted clientelist networks. Instead, under Menem's presidency (1989–1999) clientelism thrived. De la Rúa and Macri faced political opponents who mobilized those suffering from unemployment, low wages, and poverty during this period, including those who benefited from their patronage networks. Particularly in local contexts, clientelism remained prevalent across the multi-party system.

It is important to situate the case of Argentina in the context of Latin American politics, characterized by recurring economic crises, political shifts, and alternating and rather controversial development paradigms. Scholars of Latin American politics studied changes in the model of economic development that took place in the 1960s and early 1970s and observed cycles of social unrest, reforms, and enduring patterns of rent-seeking privileging the few (Chase-Dunn 1975, 723; Cardoso and Faletto 1979; Evans 1979). Between the 1930s and the 1950s, Argentina and other Latin American countries adopted policies of import-substitution industrialization (ISI) as a strategy to promote local industries by protecting them from foreign competition and to build a strong domestic market. The whole region experienced political turbulence fueled by the limitations of state-led industrialization and trade policies. The effort to foster development through import substitution actually led to economic crises, radical political agendas, and, ultimately, authoritarian backlash on several occasions.

In Argentina, the ISI policy fostered inefficient industries dependent on government protectionism. Nonetheless, this form of "developmental protectionism" was retained by Peronism as a response to the tensions created by the distributive claims of the labor forces (Cardoso and Faletto 1979: 134, 140). The Peronist governments implemented extensive social welfare programs,

---

[15] Milei's policies have had significant social impacts during his first year in power, including reduced inflation, a budget surplus, increased investor confidence and GDP growth as well as raised unemployment rates and persistent levels of poverty. They also triggered mass violent protests.

including establishing labor rights, public health care, and education reforms. They used these policies to build patronage networks, offering jobs, social benefits, and infrastructure projects in exchange for political loyalty. While this approach solidified the Peronist support base, it also entrenched corruption and inefficiency, contributed to social inequality, and hindered broader economic development (Levitsky 2003).

Protectionist policies, lack of competition, and over-reliance on government subsidies caused economic stagnation and signaled the exhaustion of the populist nationalistic paradigm in politics, which appeared to no longer address broader economic grievances. Social unrest and political instability paved the way for military coups across the region (Cardoso and Faletto 1979: 167, 174). The military regimes in Argentina, Brazil, and Chile established a *"bureaucratic-authoritarian model"* of fostering extensive industrialization led by foreign capital coupled with public investment and fiscal discipline, supported by most of the business elites and tolerated by large section of the middle class (O'Donnell 1973, 1978). Yet again, segments of the middle-class groups felt ignored and disadvantaged while industrialists felt threatened by harsh competition due to the regime's preference for international capital (O'Donnell, 1978: 8, 10).

After Argentina's return to democracy in the 1980s, the Peronist President Menem implemented sweeping reforms of privatization, trade liberalization, and decentralization between 1989 and 1999, which stabilized inflation but heightened inequality and unemployment. Menem's economic reforms were made possible, in part, by his party's under-institutionalized organizational structures, which featured fluid internal dynamics, non-bureaucratic hierarchies, and centralized leadership, enabling a degree of policy adaptability during the crises of the 1980s and 1990s (Levitsky 2003). Despite these reforms, clientelism remained pervasive throughout his presidency. The decentralization of services such as education and healthcare to provincial governments created opportunities for local politicians to distribute resources based on political loyalty, reinforcing clientelist practices at that level. Allegations of corruption during his tenure were extensive and significantly eroded trust in neoliberalism as an ideology of reform.

The Argentinean peso's peg to the US dollar, once seen as a quick fix to monetary instability, is now considered a factor that accelerated and exacerbated the 2001–2002 crisis. Argentina's fiscal and economic collapse in that crisis created a political demand for redistributive measures during recovery. Public spending resurged during the presidencies of Néstor Kirchner (2003–2007) and Cristina Fernández de Kirchner (2007–2015) who expanded social programs that were addressing poverty but also serving as tools for clientelist practices through subsidies, public sector jobs, and discretionary transfers to provinces.

Argentina's trajectory highlights the tension between reform and clientelism. Reform-oriented leaders frequently fail to meet expectations. This is because a political system is trapped in a cycle where clientelism becomes an entrenched and resurfacing phenomenon. It is beyond the capabilities of individual leaders and the skills and ideas they bring to root out clientelism as a systematic trait of politics and policy. In crises as critical junctures, political leaders are compelled to implement reforms because the system faces the risk of collapse. Yet, even in such cases, responses are frequently shaped by a *clientelist bias*, prioritizing the preservation of key networks. And, once the economy stabilizes and grows, clientelism tends to rebound.

Clientelist Bias in Policy Reform

At times, mounting debt, stagnating productivity, and growing discontent among the middle class bring political leaders before a crucial dilemma. Reforms are needed to stabilize the economy but risk alienating their clientelist bases. Can two political parties equally steeped in clientelism reach an agreement for self-restraint and reform to cancel out losses?

Geddes (1994) argues that when patronage is evenly distributed among major parties, legislators may support reforms to reduce clientelism because the losses would be shared equally while the benefits would enhance the reformers' popularity. Conversely, if patronage is unevenly distributed, parties with greater access to patronage have a weaker incentive to support reform unless the gains from reform outweigh the costs of losing patronage, such as in cases of public outrage.

However, what this analysis overlooks is that, while an agreement would help preserve a relative balance between the two parties, clientelism remains important for the internal cohesion of each party, disciplining opportunistic behavior among aspiring party cadres, deterring splits, and preventing defections. In my analysis, these parties would face problems of timing, coordination, and internal cohesion (Trantidis 2016a). First, any expected improvement from reform will come much later and will not possibly outweigh the immediate and tangible losses for the party in government. Second, the effects of reducing clientelism will not be evenly distributed between the ruling and opposition parties. The ruling party will suffer more from its own reforms that restrain clientelist supply, as the opposition could seek to mobilize its client base and may win clients from the government party by promising to resume patronage. In addition, any attempt by the government to cut or reduce the distribution of clientelist benefits poses a significant risk for its internal cohesion, risking alienating client groups who can defect to the opposition or confront the party leadership. Hence, even in conditions of crisis, both parties remain locked in a clientelist game where neither has an incentive to reduce patronage unilaterally or in an agreement with each other.

While there is strong pressure for policy reform, the political parties are trapped in the clientelist game and behave as if they were in a kind of prisoner's dilemma situation – where two players acting in their own self-interest do not communicate, or cannot communicate, to coordinate their responses to produce the optimal outcome for the group as a whole, which is making the economic system viable. Each party fears that the other would go for the collectively suboptimal option: carry on with clientelism even if it brings, accelerates, or worsens an economic and fiscal crisis. The sustainability of the economy is crucial for the stability of the clientelist system itself, but the government may choose to refrain from sweeping reforms for fear that the opposition will "defect" in the ways described above as the clientelist game. Despite signs of an incoming crisis, both parties will remain committed to maintaining and even expanding their clientelist networks when possible. The equilibrium remains stable: continue with clientelism, even when reforms are needed.

What is more, in a competitive political environment, a politician's reputation for clientelism is more of an asset than a liability even in times of crisis, as this helps them retain their clients and recruit new ones, even when their party is in the opposition. Demonstrating a consistent record of satisfied clients, especially in tough economic and fiscal conditions, enhances their credibility and appeal during the crisis and in the years ahead.

So, what happens when a crisis hits the economy? The government has a "hot potato" in its hand. Given the pressures of the clientelist system, they are better off reforming the economy in ways that preserve and spare key channels of clientelist supply to key supporters as much as possible while spreading the costs of adjustment across the general population (Trantidis 2016a). During an economic crisis, when reforming the economy becomes unavoidable, the government must creatively and skillfully balance the need to mitigate the reform impact on its client base. For instance, strict monetary policy and fiscal consolidation in the form of higher taxes or austerity cuts would spread the costs of adjustment across the population. Raising taxes for the purpose of fiscal consolidation rather than cutting expenditure will preserve clientelist supply. In short, the logic of concentrated benefits and diffused costs also works in cases of economic reform.

The Case of Greece

Greece provides an example of how the clientelist game unfolds during periods of economic and fiscal crisis. Leading a center-right *New Democracy* government during a fiscal crisis in the early 1990s, and coming from a political tradition steeped in clientelism, the government of Constantinos Mitsotakis (1990–1993) aimed to implement market-oriented reforms, reduce inefficiencies, and curb public spending. However, resistance from entrenched interests and from within his own party, including affiliated unionists in the public sector affected by his privatization agenda, derailed his plans. The defection of party MPs, shortly before the planned privatization of the state-owned telecommunications company (OTE), led to the government's fall in 1993. Mitsotakis' tenure highlights the great difficulty of promoting a reform agenda that threatens key components of a patronage-based system. For subsequent governments, Mitsotakis's experience became a cautionary tale about the risks of pursuing radical reforms. (Trantidis 2014b).

The reform trajectory under Prime Minister Costas Simitis (1996–2004) demonstrates how a clientelist party navigates pressures for political survival in a system dependent on patronage (Trantidis 2016a). The center-left *PASOK* government under the premiership of Simitis pursued fiscal consolidation and partial privatizations to meet the famous (or notorious) Maastricht criteria of low deficits and debt ceiling as a prerequisite for Greece and all other EU countries to join the European Monetary Union (EMU). The government made an effort to stabilize public finances and revamp the economy while maintaining patronage supply to PASOK's clientelist base. Simitis achieved economic stability and good growth rates without fundamentally disrupting the clientelist networks within the party, but fiscal mismanagement and entrenched clientelism continued to shape Greece's political and economic landscape, and contributed to the deteriorating fiscal conditions that brought Greece on the brink of bankruptcy in 2010.

Led by Alexis Tsipras, the left-wing party *Syriza* won the 2015 election amidst a severe economic crisis, with high levels of unemployment and a sharp decline of incomes and living standards in Greece fuelling public dissatisfaction with the two mainstream parties, PASOK and New Democracy. Promising to bring transparency, restore incomes as much as possible, rebuild the welfare state, and put an end to austerity, Alexis Tsipras formed a coalition with a smaller right-wing party to renegotiate the terms of Greece's bailout programme with the European Union (EU). Following a clash and a compromise in the summer of 2015, Tsipras embarked on stabilizing the economy following a new agreement with Greece's institutional lenders. Under their supervision, Tsipras's government achieved fiscal stabilization, reduced deficits, enacted pension and tax reforms, and stabilized the banking system.

Unlike his predecessors, Tripras made use of, and largely exhausted, the political capital he had initially enjoyed as an outsider of the bipartisan system of PASOK and New Democracy, which his supporters and several other Greeks considered responsible for the crisis. Yet, despite his government's accomplishments, many of his voters felt disillusioned with the austerity policy and the structural reforms required by Tsipras's agreement with the EU and the International Monetary Fund. At the same time, business actors and media owners aligned themselves with Kyriakos Mitsotakis, son of the former Prime Minister Constantinos Mitsotakis, in anticipation of pro-business reforms as well as clientelist benefits. *Syriza* lost the 2019 election and suffered a bigger electoral defeat in 2023. Soon after, Tsipras resigned, Syriza split, and the party's popularity significantly plummeted.

The rise and fall of Syriza illustrates the trajectory of an outsider who sought to disrupt foundational principles of a system but compromised in face of pressing realities under intense international pressure and supervision, and implemented reforms that stabilized the government budget and revamped the economy. Raising high expectations on social justice and deep political reform at the beginning, and failing to deliver on them, the party disillusioned many of its supporters despite a solid record of economic management toward the end of its tenure.

Greece's return to relative economic normality happened under the Mitsotakis government but has been accompanied with accusations of the government resuming clientelism on a large scale and building a quasi-monopolistic and dominant system of favoritism and corruption toward business interests and party supporters, particularly by granting government contracts to political allies in business, subsidies to prospective voters, and generous financial aid to media outlets.

Concluding Remarks

Is a crisis an opportunity for reform? Reform is a sort of public good. It seems that a crisis can serve as an opportunity for political leaders – usually outsiders – to capitalize upon and gain power to restructure the clientelist system. But political actors continue to rely on clientelism to solve a collective action problem, as distributing selective benefits has a greater impact on political mobilization than the supply of public goods in general.

When reform is inevitable in view of an economic crisis, policy adjustments and structural reforms may be enacted, but most likely they will be carefully designed and implemented to uphold and later revamp the clientelist system, ensuring that loyal constituencies continue to receive some benefits even amidst the general backdrop of economic restructuring. Rather than being dismantled, clientelism evolves to adjust to new economic realities and resurfaces once economic conditions are stabilized, a demonstration of this practice's embeddedness in politics and society.

Political systems tend to relapse to clientelism once the reforms implemented bring some stability and some improvement in the economy and the public finances. This pattern resembles the myth of Sisyphus in Greek mythology. Sisyphus angered the gods by cheating death and violating the sacred laws of hospitality, and Zeus condemned him to eternal punishment for this hubris: to roll a massive rock up a hill, only for it to roll back down each time he neared the top, forcing him to start over again and again. This myth can be seen as an allegory for a clientelist society: in conditions of crisis, a society must endure painful reforms but after the economy stabilizes, the governing party will revamp and expand the clientelist system at the earliest opportunity, potentially leading to new crises ahead. Any progress from the reforms will be quickly reversed. As politics and society roll back to the same clientelist game that brought up the previous crisis, pursuing reforms in a clientelist system is indeed a *Sisyphean task*.

12 Can Institutions Curb Clientelism?

The previous chapter asked a question. Can political outsiders curb clientelism? Lamentably, the answer seems to be that voters must curb their own enthusiasm instead when it comes to what they can expect from these political cavaliers. However, if clientelism is a structural trait of politics, it may be the case that institutional reforms may be the way to curb this practice. Institutional design has an enduring effect. Unlike political shooting stars and demagogues, institutions have a more profound effect. The capacity of political and socioeconomic actors to engage in clientelist exchange is shaped by what the institutional framework allows for. Can robust rule-of-law institutions effectively and sustainably limit the scope for clientelism?

What We Expect from Institutions

The defining characteristic of liberal democracy is that it is a rule-of-law system where constitutional checks and balances safeguard individual rights and liberties. These safeguards prevent the abuse of state power and ensure that political power is not concentrated in the hands of a minority or a dominant faction, regardless of their electoral strength. The government enacts laws and executes decisions in conformity with a set of constitutional rules of process – the formal rules of the game – and individual rights protecting several spheres of personal freedom. Besides elections, the separation of powers between the legislative, the executive, and the judiciary is a fundamental principle designed to prevent the concentration of state power in any single branch of government. This ensures that the government operates within a system of checks and balances, where different branches have distinct responsibilities and can hold each other accountable. Here, state power is supposed to be divided and subjected to checks by independent authorities such as the judiciary.

Public Choice theory has underpinned and stylized the development of a strand of constitutional political economy that highlights the role of baseline institutional rules, such as the US Constitution, to moderate and tame opportunistic behavior that could otherwise lead to abuses of state power. In Public Choice theory, utility maximization does not necessarily generate a dark Hobbesian world. The premise of utility maximization does not preclude the pursue of ideological beliefs and the desire to serve broader constituencies or a vision of public interest. Common concerns, such as the desire to check political power, can theoretically lead to agreements on institutional constraints on opportunistic behavior and the creation of constitutional norms that prevent the full capture and abuse of political power by majorities or minorities.

The pivotal work of Buchanan and Tullock (1962) describes this constitutional design as the rational choice of citizens concerned with preventing the prospect of majorities dominating minorities. This agreement emerges from rational actors' understanding of the mutual gains of collective norm-making. Here, Public Choice demonstrates both the limitations of democratic processes and the democratic capacity for reform. It emphasizes that individuals respond rationally to the incentives shaped by the prevailing institutional context, and places hope in rational actors agreeing on institutions that can be beneficial to society, structuring and constraining opportunistic behavior. Central to this expectation are rational calculations and, again, *a logic of exchange* where interactions resemble a contractual environment ideally leading to constitutional norms that prevent or curtail key pathologies and risks associated with politics and state power.

Indeed, the US Constitution can be interpreted as an intra-elite agreement by the Founders to prevent the tyranny of the majority in their nascent republic by way of creating a strong constitution with constraints on state power, checks and balances in government, and a bill of rights for citizens. This institutional arrangement worked well for those included in that republic as citizens and prevented formal concentrations of power. It also inspired excluded minorities and groups to strive for inclusion and equal rights, using the language of the constitution as their strongest currency in their struggles, as in the Civil Rights movement.

Still, factions remain a persistent feature of particularistic politics. in Federalist Paper 10, Madison (1961/1787) presented the problem of factions: "a number of citizens, whether amounting to a majority or a minority of the whole, who are united and actuated by some common impulse of passion, or of interest, adverse to the rights of other citizens, or to the permanent and aggregate interests of the community." Madison recognized the presence of diverse interests and social classes within a political society, and believed that the division of society into various factions alone could prevent any single faction from dominating others, particularly in large republics. He viewed civil society as a safeguard against political tyranny, asserting that ambition must be made to counteract ambition.

The US Constitution defined the rules of the political game and created institutional structures that helped prevent a leadership backed by a majority from imposing its will and oppress minorities. It remains, however, less effective in limiting the expansion of political intervention in the economy in a discretionary way that raises the stakes of politics for society and business, and still allows for particularistic politics and clientelist exchange.

So, there is scope for further institutional redesigning to place new checks on political power and, consequently, further limit the discretionary use of public resources through patronage. Starting with a truly independent judiciary, merit-based civil service recruitment and transparent procurement processes, the reform direction should be toward creating a stronger, rule-based framework of governance that establishes generality as a core constitutional principle in economic policy so as to protect the system from favoritism, inefficiency, and social discord from the pursuit of special interests (Buchanan and Congleton 1998). Designing a principle of generality for policymaking must now find novel ways to restrict governments from indulging in politics driven by special interests.

Is this Kind of Constitutional Reform Likely?

Can a process of constitutional reform generate better institutions to curb the practice of clientelism? The distinction between constitutional rules (institutional order) and policymaking is important: it lies in the superior and structuring position of institutions versus ordinary politics and policymaking. Institutional reforms change the "rules of the game" by reshaping incentives and creating enduring constraints, while policies are the game constrained by these baseline rules.

Here comes the idea of a state and of a public administration imbued with Weberian-like qualities, characterized by impartiality, professionalism, and autonomy as an appealing institutional solution to the problem of clientelism.[16]

---

[16] For instance, Shefter (1977) argues that whether party leaders choose clientelist or programmatic voter-mobilization strategies depends on two institutional parameters: The relative timing of bureaucratization (the development of a rational administrative system) and democratization (the introduction of universal male suffrage) in that country.

The question, however, is whether we can plausibly expect that this direction of constitutional reform will ever occur. In that regard, the process of constitutional design and institutional reform can be examined in light of the problem of collective action (Olson 1965) and the logic of political action that underpins the practice of clientelism.

As the previous chapters demonstrate, clientelism generates pressures for governments to expand, rather than limit, the scope of clientelism. The clientelist system generates an in-built policy bias in favor of this type of politics and will likely exhibit strong resistance to institutional reform for the very same reason there is resistance to economic reforms: client groups are vital resources for the parties alternating in government. Both the government and the opposition are trapped in a game in which they must safeguard the institutional environment that will secure the viability of the clientelist system.

logic of exchange invites clientelist agreements at the stage of constitutional design. Institutions are not neutral; they determine the permissible range and forms of state actions, define and limit property rights, and regulate social and economic activities. Institutional norms and processes have clear distributional consequences, they inevitably create entrenched categories of winners and losers, often embedding benefits for some in the system while systemically disadvantaging others. This dynamic can generate competition and diverse pressures for reform during a stage of constitutional revision (Trantidis 2017). Consequently, individuals and groups with important stakes in terms of how these foundational rules should be configured will mobilize to reform and reconfigure these institutions in their favor. In those rare circumstances, they will actively try to promote their interests in the form of proposals for constitutional rules.

The stakes are higher than ordinary politics because, unlike competing for distributions and the occasional favor, they are now competing for the rules of the game that will entrench a distributional bias, knowing that the opportunity for later constitutional revision may never come again during their lifetime. Rules that determine the structure of the system itself embed privileges and establish patterns of advantage over long periods of time, making them far more consequential than temporary policy shifts and gains. As such, constitutional reform and institutional design are processes not detached from the same incentives that shape the circumstances of politics as particularistic and clientelist. If core norms of the political and institutional system are to be negotiated and agreed upon, there is already a dominant strategy for the major stakeholders: to engage in clientelist exchange with the constitutional legislators and embed privileges for them in the constitutional order.

Institutions, Informal Relations and Clientelism

The book's analysis has placed great emphasis not just on formal rules but also on the personal, informal channels of interaction, communication, influence, and bargaining between their members and those in power, which permeate these formal divisions. Even when there is a constitutional framework with checks and balances such as a formally independent judiciary, the underlying logic of exchange that fosters clientelism remains present in the informal and personal relations and networks that inhabit the institutional system. The logic of exchange that sustains patronage relations in areas such as politics and business also influences strategies and the real autonomy of those in charge of these institutions in relation to those with the political power to distribute resources and economic and social opportunities. Simply dividing state power among different branches of government cannot thwart the incentives for actors to engage with and join structures of privilege.

For example, judges and members of independent authorities, such as central banks, are often seen as neutral arbiters of law and policy, tasked with maintaining impartiality and ensuring the integrity of the legal and economic system. However, office holders in those institutions are not immune to the allure of clientelist benefits. They may have or wish to build connections with political networks. They may already come from families with longstanding political affiliations who sponsored their careers. Through these relationships, they often cultivate personal ties and political loyalties that extend beyond their formal responsibilities and benefit from informal channels of influence and promotion. For example, some judges or leaders of independent authorities or their relatives and spouses may have personal or family connections to businesses that stand to gain from patronage or state contracts.

The line of formal independence among power centers is porous and permeable by informal associations and clientelist ties that can seep into organizations that are designed to act impartially and safeguard the public good. Even though institutions may be structured to function independently in theory, the influence of personal connections can undermine their real autonomy. The pressures from these networks can sway decisions, distort priorities, and ultimately weaken the institutions' capacity to act impartially.

Clientelist networks can thus penetrate civil society, actively discouraging and deterring the emergence of alternative, autonomous spheres of activity that could challenge the dominance of a clientelist party: NGO's, journalists, think tanks, academic circles, etc. All spheres of social activity, from civil society to the various functions of government, host complex networks of interactions where the distribution of resources – "who gets what, when, and how" – is often determined by personal connections and clientelist ties to powerful political figures. These clientelist relationships undermine the autonomy of civil society institutions, journalists, and activists.

The landscape of institutions and actors under clientelism may come as far as resembling more of a cartel than a pluralistic society governed by the rule of law. This environment perpetuates a system of privilege and exclusion, where, on one side, there are the many citizens who have little influence over political decision-making, and on the other side, there are the few "insiders" who maintain relationships with political patrons, influential clients, and organizations, hold key roles in both the public and private sectors, and keep extracting benefits due to clientelist exchange and patronage networks in various capacities, often capitalizing from their position as judges, parliamentarians, senior civil servants or journalists.

Concluding Remarks

For the question "Can robust rule-of-law institutions effectively and sustainably limit the scope for clientelism?" the answer is to remind us that the logic of exchange is present in constitutional politics too as much as in the pre-constitutional and post-constitutional system. Clientelist deals between powerful economic and political actors may govern the stage of constitutional design and define the new institutional rules. Those with important stakes in shaping the content of these rules will use their personal connections and develop patronage ties in order to influence constitutional outcomes the same way they seek to influence policymaking. Worse, in those rare moments of constitutional design, antagonistic groups and competing politicians will set aside their differences and unite in safeguarding or expanding an institutional structure that will allow them to compete for special benefits or clients, respectively. Their shared goal would be about maintaining the type of institutions that enable and protect the supply of clientelism, regardless of their substantive differences and antagonisms for those clientelist benefits, even if they may later clash with one another over who gets these benefits and even if their clientelist alliances differ.

This is not to say that institutions don't matter. They determine the extent to which political actors have the license to develop clientelist exchanges and the room to expand them. However, institutions are not insuperable constraints on political behavior, and they do not stand above the circumstances of politics. Institutions and constitutions are not exogenous to the political and economic relations that have developed in society, including the power asymmetries and opportunistic incentives of clientelist politics. As noted earlier, the logic of political action and the logic of exchange favor the development of a clientelist system and the weakening of independent institutions. In that regard, the practice of clientelism both prevents taking the kind of reform that will seriously curb clientelism as well as undermines the independence of the institutions that are supposed to promote equal treatment, fair representation, public transparency, and political accountability. The self-reinforcing dynamic of clientelism is difficult, if not impossible to break.

There seems to be a paradox with the state and its institutions: the state as an organization is meant to uphold law and order in an organized society but its own unmatched power and capacity simultaneously generate the conditions that weaken the autonomy of society and the capacity of the state institutions themselves to act independently as safeguards of that law and order in suitably impersonal terms. The system that state institutions create and manage, in fact, invites competition among self-interested actors over both the baseline rules and binding government decisions that distribute benefits and costs. Consequently, state institutions are shaped and configured by asymmetrical political power relations, including informal networks with their relative recruitment and mobilizing capacity. The idea of a state entirely autonomous from clientelism, rent-seeking, and corruption is a utopian vision.

13 Concluding Remarks

This book started by tackling the conceptual problem of defining and understanding clientelism. Previous research, particularly in ethnography and political science, has studied clientelism as a practice primarily involving voters. The focus was on poorer regions and societies in Africa, Latin America, and Southern and Eastern Europe. Understandably, this focus on very obvious and widespread practices led to a narrow conception of clientelism, which inadvertently excludes manifestations of clientelist exchange in advanced democracies and richer economies like those in Europe and the United States, and fails to highlight the systemic presence and effect which clientelism has in all these societies.

The book demonstrates why clientelism is a pervasive and impactful phenomenon across democracies, including advanced economies, due to the way state power intersects with society and the way social, economic, and political actors respond to it, motivated by *the logic of exchange* prevalent in all forms of human interaction. From here, it analyses the impact of patronage on the terms of political competition, the choice of preferences and interests to be satisfied through policymaking as a priority, how it undermines the principle of political equality, how it produces systemic effects on economic policy, distorts economic institutions and undermines economic activity and, in some cases, how it could facilitate the rise of dominant political forces against a weak civil society.

First, in revisiting clientelism, the book uncovers the incentive structure that explains why clientelism occurs. Clientelist exchanges provide personal rewards that significantly improve the clients' individual circumstances such as their financial situation, social standing, businesses, and career progression. These benefits are selective, substantial, often exclusive, and personalized. Just as the typical private goods one gets from market activities motivate private investment plans and productive activities, clientelist benefits similarly motivate people to get involved in political activities.

Second, the book conceptualizes political competition as consisting of *two games*. The first game is about political parties and politicians gathering campaign resources and active supporters to organize their campaign, and clientelism serves as a method of *campaign organization for electoral mobilization*. The second game is electoral competition, where those resources are employed to promote programmatic messages and appeal to the general public. Political parties and candidates who engage in clientelism gain an advantage in campaign resources and political organization and, subsequently, an advantage in addressing the broader public and attracting voters. They need to recruit active supporters who would dedicate a lot of time and energy in their political campaign as well as donors who would give large sums of money as a campaign donation. These actors would agree to offer sizeable contributions insofar as what they get, in return, a benefit that is substantial enough to far outweigh the cost of their contribution; one that significantly improves their own personal circumstances and offers additional benefits exclusive to them.

Hence, the electoral game is *nested* in the clientelist game. Politicians and political organizations must obtain the resources to organize a campaign and address the broader electorate. This objective is a necessary condition for political survival and electoral success because the distribution of campaign resources among political competitors affects, even if it does not determine, the chances of political parties and politicians for political survival and electoral success.

It has also been highlighted that clientelism provides a solution to the collective action problem regarding the organization of a political party as a large and relatively heterogeneous group of people. Clientelism helps leaders transform a diverse and often rambling political group into a more disciplined and coordinated organization. Here, clientelism not only mobilizes contributions but also reduces internal divisions within political parties. Selective incentives help party leaders maintain party discipline by rewarding loyalty and by punishing dissent, defection, and free-riding with exclusion from these benefits. This way, they can minimize internal fragmentation and restrict the likelihood of party cadres and party members voicing discontent or even challenging their leadership. Clientelism is therefore "the glue that binds" career politicians with personal aspirations and opportunistic strategies as well as those who are ideologues or wish to gain the opportunity to serve in a public office and promote the causes they care about.

In short, this book provides a necessary complement to what is missing from Public Choice theory and from its approach to democratic systems and policymaking. *The logic of political action* is a much-needed extension to the literature on rent-seeking and Olson's analysis of the logic of collective action, by explaining why smaller groups not only organize collective action easier but can also be effective in terms of securing the policy benefits they claim, even in democratic systems in which politicians are supposed to be responsive to the preferences of the majority or their selectorate. In other words, Olson highlighted dynamics on the demand side of policy – mobilization of special interest groups – while this book provides a detailed analysis of the supply side of politics – why politicians will indeed prioritize catering for these special interests.

Implications for the Study of Democratic Governance

Clientelism, thoroughly analyzed and understood, reveals the large distance separating actual politics and ideal-type representations of democratic politics. A deeper study of clientelism challenges the assertion that, in a democracy, the proportion of public goods provided will outweigh private goods to a few by the government because of the large size of the support base the leader needs to win in order to get elected and the high cost of providing private goods to this group (cf. the "selectorate" in the words of Bruce Bueno de Mesquita et al. 2003). In reality, in democracies, the clientelist network is for the political party in government, the "pre-selectorate," the group which it must satisfy first so that the governing party and its politicians can gain enough resources to appeal to general voters. A democratic system is supposed to enable all citizens to engage in political processes and various forms of political participation, but extensive networks of patronage make it easier for some to advance their personal interests by selling their time and energy or by trading some of their resources.

This entrenches a *clientelist bias* in policymaking and runs counter to normative representations of democracy and the analytical and idealized images of government in the disciplines of economics and public administration. In reality, a functioning democracy is *still* an elite structure with a few privileged groups that tend to dominate the policy agenda. Access to decision-making and policymaking is significantly shaped by informal interactions at the elite level, often taking the form of clientelist exchanges across patronage networks. At the same time, those few political parties and politicians that have established sizeable clientelist networks raise significant barriers to entry for potential rivals. This situation may go as far as infusing democracy with characteristics that resemble those of an oligarchy.

Moreover, while extensive clientelism is happening in the hidden background, public debates over policy, including electoral campaigns and party manifestos, continue to reproduce the idea of public goods provision and invoke the norm of political equality. In that regard, politics becomes a "market for lemons" where a few political actors promote policy agendas to citizens that hide from the public the main reason they were designed: to yield benefits to clients and to themselves. These policies are "sold" to voters by framing them positively as serving a public purpose. The problem of asymmetrical information is thus related to the asymmetries in resources for political organization and campaign, not necessarily voters' ignorance or apathy.

In sharp contrast to ideal conceptions of government, democracies entail strong incentives, and offer opportunities for the systemic extraction of special benefits by few at the expense of society and the economy. The essence of politics is inherently competitive and fundamentally distributional. The logic of exchange in politics arises precisely from this reality, and clientelism emerges at the intersection of political and economic competition, creating a system of privilege for a select few. This practice also engulfs democracy's baseline institutions and even the workings and design of a constitution itself that assigns rights in the first place. Formal institutions host opportunistic actors, and are permeated by informal networks of personal and often clientelistic connections, while any reform opportunities along the way invite contestation driven by the same logic.

Clientelism is thus not an exception to the democratic standard of political behavior; it is not a pathology of the workings of politics and government. It is part of the physiology of politics and, ultimately, of a society defined by a logic of exchange that governs all types of human interactions, generating patterns of competition and collaboration, collusion and co-option. Where there is politics, there is clientelism.

References

Acemoglu, Daron, and James A. Robinson. 2012. *Why Nations Fail: The Origins of Power, Prosperity, and Poverty*. New York: Crown Business.

Achen, Christopher H., and Larry M. Bartels. 2016. *Democracy for Realists: Why Elections Do Not Produce Responsive Government*. Princeton, NJ: Princeton University Press.

Aldrich, John H. 1995. *Why Parties? The Origin and Transformation of Political Parties in America*. Chicago, IL: University of Chicago Press.

Aligica, Paul Dragoş, and Vlad Tarko. 2015. *Capitalist Alternatives: Models, Taxonomies, Scenarios*. London: Routledge.

Arrow, Kenneth J. 1951. *Social Choice and Individual Values*. New Haven, CT: Yale University Press.

Auyero, Javier. 1999. "From the Client's Point(s) of View: How Poor People Perceive and Evaluate Political Clientelism." *Theory and Society* 28(2): 297–334.

Banfield, Edward C. 1958. *The Moral Basis of a Backward Society*. Glencoe: Free Press.

Barber, Mark J., Brandice Canes-Wrone, and Sarah Sharece Thrower. 2017. "Ideologically Sophisticated Donors: Which Candidates Do Individual Contributors Finance?" *American Journal of Political Science* 61(2): 271–288.

Bartels, Larry M. 2008. *Unequal Democracy: The Political Economy of the New Gilded Age*. Princeton, NJ: Princeton University Press.

Boettke, Peter J., and Henry A. Thompson. 2019. "Identity and Off-Diagonals: How Permanent Winning Coalitions Destroy Democratic Governance." *Public Choice* 191(3–4): 483–499.

Boettke, Peter J., Christopher J. Coyne, and Peter T. Leeson. 2005. "Institutional Stickiness and the New Development Economics." *The American Journal of Economics and Sociology* 67(2): 331–358.

Bonica, Adam. 2013. "Ideology and Interests in the Political Marketplace." *American Journal of Political Science* 57(2): 294–311.

Brady, Henry E., Sidney Verba, and Kay Lehman Schlozman. 1995. "Beyond SES: A Resource Model of Political Participation." *American Political Science Review* 89(2): 271–294.

Buchanan, James M. 1972. "Toward Analysis of Closed Behavioral Systems." In *Theory of Public Choice: Political Applications of Economics*, edited by

James M. Buchanan and Robert D. Tollison, 11–23. Ann Arbor, MI: University of Michigan Press

Buchanan, James. 2000. *The Collected Works of James M. Buchanan: Volume 1 – The Logical Foundations of Constitutional Liberty.* Indianapolis, IN: Liberty Fund.

Buchanan, James, and Gordon Tullock. 1962. *The Calculus of Consent: Logical Foundations of Constitutional Democracy.* Ann Arbor: University of Michigan Press.

Buchanan, James M., and Geoffrey Brennan. 1985. *The Reason of Rules: Three Essays in Political Theory.* Indianapolis, IN: Liberty Fund.

Buchanan, James M., and Roger D. Congleton. 1998. *Politics by Principle, Not Interest: Towards Nondiscriminatory Democracy.* Cambridge: Cambridge University Press.

Bueno de Mesquita, Bruce, Alastair Smith, Randolph M. Siverson, and James Morrow D. 2003. *The Logic of Political Survival.* Cambridge, MA: MIT Press.

Camp, Elizabeth. 2017. "Cultivating Effective Brokers: A Party Leader's Dilemma." *British Journal of Political Science* 47(3): 521–543.

Caplan, Bryan. 2007. *The Myth of the Rational Voter: Why Democracies Choose Bad Policies.* Princeton, NJ: Princeton University Press.

Cardoso, Fernando H., and Ernesto Faletto. 1979. *Dependency and Development in Latin America.* Berkeley: University of California Press.

Chandra, Kanchan. 2004. *Why Ethnic Parties Succeed: Patronage and Ethnic Head Counts in India.* Cambridge: Cambridge University Press.

Chase-Dunn, Christopher. 1975. "The Effects of International Economic Dependence on Development and Inequality." *American Sociological Review* 40(6): 720–739.

Chubb, Judith. 1982. *Patronage, Power, and Poverty in Southern Italy: A Tale of Two Cities.* Cambridge: Cambridge University Press.

Cowen, Nick, Eric Schliesser, and Aris Trantidis. 2025. "Democracy as a Competitive Discovery Process." *European Journal of Political Economy.* Advance online publication. https://doi.org/10.1016/j.ejpoleco.2025.102695.

Cox, Gary W. 1997. *Making Votes Count: Strategic Coordination in the World's Electoral Systems.* Cambridge: Cambridge University Press.

Cox, Gary W. 1999. "Electoral Rules and Electoral Coordination." *Annual Review of Political Science* 2: 145–161.

Cox, Gary W., and Michael F. Thies. 1998. "The Cost of Intraparty Competition: The Single, Nontransferable Vote and Money Politics in Japan." *Comparative Political Studies* 31(3): 267–291.

Cruz, Cesi, and Philip Keefer. 2015. "Political Parties, Clientelism, and Bureaucratic Reform." *Comparative Political Studies* 48(14): 1942–1973.

Dahl, Robert A. 1971. *Polyarchy: Participation and Opposition*. New Haven, CT: Yale University.

Della Porta, Donatella. 2020. *How Social Movements Can Save Democracy: Democratic Innovations from Below*. Cambridge: Polity.

Della Porta, Donatella, and Alberto Vannucci. 1999. *Corrupt Exchanges: Actors, Resources, and Mechanisms of Political Corruption*. New York: Aldine de Gruyter.

Denzau, Arthur T., and Michael C. Munger. 1986. "Legislators and Interest Groups: How Unorganized Interests Get Represented." *American Political Science Review* 80(1): 89–106.

Desai, Mihir, Rajeev Singh, Thomas Janoski et al. 2020. "Machine Politics and Clientelism." In Cecilia de Leon, Ian W. Martin, Joya Misra et al. (eds.) *The New Handbook of Political Sociology*. Cambridge: Cambridge University Press, pp. 666–680.

Dixit, Avinash K., and John B. Londregan. 1996. "The Determinants of Success of Special Interests in Redistributive Politics." *Journal of Politics* 58(4): 1132–1155.

Downs, Anthony. 1957. *An Economic Theory of Democracy*. New York: Harper and Row.

Eisenstadt, Shmuel N., and Luis Roniger. 1980. "Patron–Client Relations as a Model of Structuring Social Exchange." *Comparative Studies in Society and History* 22(1): 42–77.

Eisenstadt, Shmuel N., and Luis Roniger. 1984. *Patrons, Clients and Friends: Interpersonal Relations and the Structure of Trust in Society*. Cambridge: Cambridge University Press.

Evans, Peter. 1979. *Dependent Development: The Alliance of Multinational State and Local Capital in Brazil*. Princeton, NJ: Princeton University Press.

Evans, Peter. 1992. "The State as Problem and Solution: Predation, Embedded Autonomy, and Structural Change." In *The Politics of Economic Adjustment: International Constraints, Distributive Conflicts, and the State*, edited by Stephan Haggard and Robert R. Kaufman, 139–181. Princeton, NJ: Princeton University Press.

Fouirnaies, Alexander 2021. "How Do Campaign Spending Limits Affect Elections? Evidence from the United Kingdom 1885–2019." *American Political Science Review* 115(2): 395–411.

Gans-Morse, Jordan, Sebastián Mazzuca, and Simeon Nichter. 2014. "Varieties of Clientelism: Machine Politics during Elections." *American Journal of Political Science* 58(2): 415–432.

Geddes, Barbara. 1994. *Politician's Dilemma*. Berkeley: University of California Press.

Gellner, Ernest, and John Waterbury (eds.) 1977. *Patrons and Clients in Mediterranean Societies*. London: Duckworth.

Gherghina, Sergiu, and Clara Volintiru. 2017. "A New Model of Clientelism: Political Parties, Public Resources, and Private Contributors." *European Political Science Review* 9(1): 115–137.

Gilens, Martin, and Benjamin I. Page. 2014. "Testing Theories of American Politics: Elites, Interest Groups, and Average Citizens." *Perspectives on Politics* 12(3): 564–581.

Golden, Martin A. 2003. "Electoral Connections: The Effects of the Personal Vote on Political Patronage, Bureaucracy, and Legislation in Postwar Italy." *British Journal of Political Science* 33(2): 189–212.

Graziano, Paolo. 1973. "Patron-Client Relationships in Southern Italy." *European Journal of Political Research* 1(1): 3–34.

Grossman, Gene M., and Elhanan Helpman. 1994. "Protection for Sale." *American Economic Review* 84(4): 833–850.

Grossman, Gene M., and Elhanan Helpman. 2001. *Special Interest Politics*. Cambridge, MA: MIT Press.

Grzymala-Busse, Anna. 2007. *Rebuilding Leviathan: Party Competition and State Exploitation in Post-Communist Democracies*. New York: Cambridge University Press.

Grzymala-Busse, Anna. 2008. "Beyond Clientelism: Incumbent State Capture and State Building." *Comparative Political Studies* 41(4–5): 638–673.

Haber, Stephen (ed.). 2002. *Crony Capitalism and Economic Growth in Latin America: Theory and Evidence*. Stanford: Hoover Institution Press.

Hacker, Jacob S., and Paul Pierson. 2010a. *Winner-Take-All Politics: How Washington Made the Rich Richer – and Turned Its Back on the Middle Class*. New York: Simon & Schuster.

Hacker, Jacob S., and Paul Pierson. 2010b. "Winner-Take-All Politics: Public Policy, Political Organization, and the Precipitous Rise of Top Incomes in the United States." *Politics & Society* 38(2): 152–204.

Haeffele, Stephanie (ed.) 2018. *Knowledge and Incentives in Policy: Using Public Choice and Market Process Theory to Analyze Public Policy Issues*. London: Rowman & Littlefield International.

Hall, Andrew B. 2016. "Systemic Effects of Campaign Spending: Evidence from Corporate Campaign Contribution Bans in State Legislatures." *Political Science Research and Methods* 4(2): 343–359.

Hellman, Joel S., and Daniel Kaufmann. 2001. "Confronting the Challenge of State Capture in Transition Economies." *Finance & Development* 38(3): 31–35.

Hicken, Allen. 2011. "Clientelism." *Annual Review of Political Science* 14: 289–310.

Hicken, Allen, and Noah L. Nathan. 2020. "Clientelism's Red Herrings: Reducing Bias in the Study of Nonprogrammatic Politics." *Annual Review of Political Science* 23: 277–294.

Hicken, Allen, and Joel W. Simmons. 2008. "The Personal Vote and the Efficacy of Education Spending." *American Journal of Political Science* 52(1): 109–124.

Higashijima, Masaaki, and Hidekuni Washida. 2024. "Varieties of Clientelism across Political Parties: New Measures of Patron–Client Relationships." *European Political Science Review* 16(2): 260–280.

Hilgers, Tina. 2009. "'Who Is Using Whom?' Clientelism from the Client's Perspective." *Journal of Iberian and Latin American Research* 15(1): 51–75.

Holcombe, Randall G. 2018. *Political Capitalism: How Economic and Political Power Is Made and Maintained*. Cambridge: Cambridge University Press.

Hopkin, Jonathan. 2001. *Party Formation and Democratic Transition in Spain: The Creation and Collapse of the Union of the Democratic Centre*. New York: Palgrave.

Hopkin, Jonathan. 2006. "Conceptualizing Political Clientelism: Political Exchange and Democratic Theory." Paper presented at the American Political Science Association (APSA) Annual Meeting, Philadelphia, August 31–September 3.

Jacobson, Gary C. 1990. "The Effects of Campaign Spending in House Elections: New Evidence for Old Arguments." *American Journal of Political Science* 34(2): 334–362.

Katz, Richard S., and Peter Mair. 1995. "Changing Models of Party Organization and Party Democracy: The Emergence of the Cartel Party." *Party Politics* 1(1): 5–28.

Kaufman, Robert R. 1974. "The Patron-Client Concept and Macro-Politics: Prospects and Problems." *Comparative Studies in Society and History* 16 (3): 284–308.

Keefer, Philip. 2007. "Clientelism, Credibility, and the Policy Choices of Young Democracies." *American Journal of Political Science* 51(4): 804–821.

Keefer, Philip, and Razvan Vlaicu. 2008. "Democracy, Credibility, and Clientelism." *Journal of Law, Economics, and Organization* 24 (2): 371–406

Khan, Mushtaq H., and Kwame Sundaram Jomo (eds.). 2000. *Rents, Rent-Seeking and Economic Development*. Cambridge: Cambridge University Press.

Kitschelt, Herbert. 2000. "Citizens, Politicians, and Party Cartellization: Political Representation and State Failure in Post-Industrial Democracies." *European Journal of Political Research* 37: 149–179.

Kitschelt, Herbert. 2007. "The Demise of Clientelism in Affluent Capitalist Democracies." In *Patrons, Clients, and Policies: Patterns of Democratic Accountability and Political Competition*, edited by Herbert Kitschelt and Steven I. Wilkinson, 298–321. Cambridge: Cambridge University Press.

Kitschelt, Herbert, and Steven I. Wilkinson (eds.). 2007. *Patrons, Clients, and Policies: Patterns of Democratic Accountability and Political Competition*. Cambridge: Cambridge University Press.

Kramon, Eric. 2019. "Ethnic Group Institutions and Electoral Clientelism." *Party Politics* 25(3): 435–447.

Kroszner, Randall S., and Thomas Stratmann. 2005. "Corporate Campaign Contributions, Repeat Giving, and the Rewards to Legislator Reputation." *Journal of Law and Economics* 48(1): 41–71.

Krueger, Anne O. 1974. "The Political Economy of the Rent-Seeking Society." *American Economic Review* 64(3): 291–303.

Landé, Carl H. 1977. "Introduction: The Dyadic Basis of Clientelism." In *Friends, Followers, and Factions: A Reader in Political Clientelism*, edited by Steffen W. Schmidt, Laura Guasti, Carl H. Landé, and James C. Scott, xiii–xxxvii. London: University of California Press.

Landé, Carl H. 1983. "Political Clientelism in Political Studies: Retrospect and Prospects." *International Political Science Review/ Revue Internationale de Science Politique* 4(4): 435–454.

LaPalombara, Joseph. 1964. *Interest Groups in Italian Politics*. Princeton, NJ: Princeton University Press.

Legg, Kenneth. 1972. "Interpersonal Relationships and Comparative Politics: Political Clientelism in Industrial Society." *Politics* 7(1): 1–11.

Lemarchand, René. 1972. "Political Clientelism and Ethnicity in Tropical Africa: Competing Solidarities in Nation-Building." *The American Political Science Review* 66(1): 68–90.

Levitsky, Steven. 2003. *Transforming Labor-Based Parties in Latin America: The Argentine Justicialista Party in Comparative Perspective*. Cambridge: Cambridge University Press.

Lindsey, Brink, and Steven M. Teles. 2017. *The Captured Economy: How the Powerful Enrich Themselves, Slow Down Growth, and Increase Inequality*. Oxford: Oxford University Press.

Lust, Ellen. 2009. "Democratization by Elections? Competitive Clientelism in the Middle East." *Journal of Democracy* 20(3): 122–135.

Lyrintzis, Christos. 1984. "Political Parties in Post-Junta Greece: A Case of 'Bureaucratic Clientelism'?" *West European Politics* 7(2): 99–118.

Madison, James. 1961/1787. Federalist No. 10, in *The Federalist Papers*, ed. C. Rossiter. New York: New American Library.

Magaloni, Beatriz. 2006. *Voting for Autocracy: Hegemonic Party Survival and Its Demise in Mexico*. Cambridge: Cambridge University Press.

Mainwaring, Scott P. 1999. *Rethinking Party Systems in the Third Wave of Democratization: The Case of Brazil*. Stanford, CA: Stanford University Press.

Manzetti, Luigi, and Craig J. Wilson. 2007. "Why Do Corrupt Governments Maintain Public Support?" *Comparative Political Studies* 40(8): 949–970.

McCormick, Robert E., and Robert D. Tollison. 1981. *Politicians, Legislation, and the Economy: An Inquiry into the Interest-Group Theory of Government*. London: Martinus Nijhoff.

McLean, Iain 1987. *Public Choice: An Introduction*. Oxford: Basil Blackwell.

McRae, C. Duncan. 1977. "A Political Model of the Business Cycle." *Journal of Political Economy* 85: 239–263.

Medina, Leonardo R., and Susan C. Stokes. 2007. "Monopoly and Monitoring: An Approach to Political Clientelism." In *Citizen-Politician Linkages: An Introduction*, edited by Herbert Kitschelt and Steven I. Wilkinson. Cambridge: Cambridge University Press, pp. 83–88.

Mueller, Wolfgang C. 1989. *The Austrian Party System: Continuity and Change Since 1945*. Vienna: Braumüller.

Mueller, Dennis C. 2003. *Public Choice III*. Cambridge: Cambridge University Press.

Munshi, Soumyanetra. 2022. "Clientelism or Public Goods: Dilemma in a 'Divided Democracy'." *Constitutional Political Economy* 33: 483–506.

Nichter, Simeon C. 2010. *Politics and Poverty: Electoral Clientelism in Latin America*. Berkeley: University of California, PhD dissertation.

Nichter, Simeon. 2018. *Votes for Survival: Relational Clientelism in Latin America*. New York: Cambridge University Press.

Niskanen, William A. 1971. *Bureaucracy and Representative Government*. Chicago, IL: Aldine-Atherton.

Nordhaus, William D. 1975. "The Political Business Cycle." *Review of Economic Studies* 42: 169–190.

North, Douglass C., John Joseph Wallis, and Barry R. Weingast. 2009. *Violence and Social Orders: A Conceptual Framework for Interpreting Recorded Human History*. New York: Cambridge University Press.

North, Douglass C., John Joseph Wallis, Steven B. Webb, and Barry R. Weingast. 2007. *Limited Access Orders in the Developing World: A New Approach to the Problems of Development*. Washington, DC: World Bank Policy Research Working Paper No. 4359.

O'Donnell, Guillermo A. 1973. *Modernization and Bureaucratic-Authoritarianism: Studies in South American Politics*. Berkeley: Institute of International Studies, University of California.

O'Donnell, Guillermo. 1978. Reflections on the Patterns of Change in the Bureaucratic-Authoritarian State. *Latin American Research Review* 13(1): 3–38.

Olson, Mancur. 1965. *The Logic of Collective Action: Public Goods and the Theory of Groups*. Cambridge, MA: Harvard University Press.

Olson, Mancur. 2000. *Power and Prosperity: Outgrowing Communist and Capitalist Dictatorships*. New York: Basic Books.

Pellicer, Miquel, Eva Wegner, Markus Bayer, and Christian Tischmeyer. 2020. "Clientelism from the Client's Perspective: A Meta-Analysis of Ethnographic Literature." *Perspectives on Politics* 20(3): 931–947.

Peltzman, Sam. 1976. "Toward a More General Theory of Regulation." *Journal of Law and Economics* 19(2): 211–240.

Piattoni, Simona (ed.) 2001a. *Clientelism, Interests, and Democratic Representation: The European Experience in Historical and Comparative Perspective*. Cambridge: Cambridge University Press.

Piattoni, Simona. 2001b. *Clientelism in Historical and Comparative Perspective*. In Simona Piattoni (ed.) *Clientelism, Interests, and Political Representation: Theory and Evidence from Italy*. Cambridge: Cambridge University Press, pp. 1–30.

Piattoni, Simona (ed.) 2004. *Clientelism, Interests, and Democratic Representation: The European Experience in Historical and Comparative Perspective*. Cambridge: Cambridge University Press.

Pierson, Paul. 2004. *Politics in Time: History, Institutions, and Social Analysis*. Princeton, NJ: Princeton University Press.

Powell, Lynda W. 2012. *The Influence of Campaign Contributions in State Legislatures: The Effects of Institutions and Politics*. Ann Arbor: University of Michigan Press.

Putnam, Robert D. 1993. *Making Democracy Work: Civic Traditions in Modern Italy*. Princeton, NJ: Princeton University Press.

Ravanilla, Nico, and Allen Hicken. 2023. "Poverty, Social Networks, and Clientelism." *World Development* 162: 106128.

Riker, William H. 1962. *The Theory of Political Coalitions*. New Haven, CT: Yale University Press.

Robinson, James A., and Thierry Verdier. 2013. "The Political Economy of Clientelism." *Scandinavian Journal of Economics* 115(2): 260–291.

Roniger, Luis, and Ayşe Güneş-Ayata, eds. 1994. *Democracy, Clientelism, and Civil Society*. Boulder, CO: Lynne Rienner Publishers.

Schlozman, Kay Lehman, Sidney Verba, and Henry E. Brady. 2012. *The Unheavenly Chorus: Unequal Political Voice and the Broken Promise of American Democracy*. Princeton, NJ: Princeton University Press.

Schnakenberg, Kevin E., and Ian R. Turner. 2021. "Helping Friends or Influencing Foes: Electoral and Policy Effects of Campaign Finance Contributions." *American Journal of Political Science* 65: 88–100.

Scott, James C. 1972. "Patron-Client Politics and Political Change in Southeast Asia." *The American Political Science Review* 66(1): 91–113.

Shefter, Martin. 1977. "Party and Patronage: Germany, England, and Italy." *Political Society* 7: 403–451.

Somin, Ilya. 2013. *Democracy and Political Ignorance: Why Smaller Government Is Smarter*. Stanford, CA: Stanford University Press.

Somin, Ilya. 2016. *Democracy and Political Ignorance: Why Smaller Government Is Safer than Bigger Government*. Stanford, CA: Stanford University Press.

Stigler, George J. 1971. "The Theory of Economic Regulation." *The Bell Journal of Economics and Management Science* 2(1): 3–21.

Stokes, Susan C. 2005. "Perverse Accountability: A Formal Model of Machine Politics with Evidence from Argentina." *American Political Science Review* 99(3): 315–325.

Stokes, Susan C. 2007. "Political Clientelism." In Carles Boix and Susan C. Stokes (eds.) *The Oxford Handbook of Comparative Politics*. New York: Oxford University Press, pp. 604–627.

Stokes, Susan C. 2021. Clientelism and Development: Is There a Poverty Trap? WIDER Working Paper 2021/91. Helsinki: UNU-WIDER.

Stokes, Susan C., Thad Dunning, and Marcelo Nazareno. 2013. *Brokers, Voters, and Clientelism: The Puzzle of Distributive Politics*. Cambridge: Cambridge University Press.

Szwarcberg, Marcelo. 2015. *Mobilizing Poor Voters: Machine Politics, Clientelism, and Social Networks in Argentina*. Cambridge: Cambridge University Press.

Trantidis, Aris. 2014a. "Clientelism and the Classification of Dominant Party Systems." *Democratization* 22(1): 113–133.

Trantidis, Aris. 2014b. "Reforms and Collective Action in a Clientelist System: Greece during the Mitsotakis Administration (1990–93)." *South European Society and Politics* 19(2): 215–234.

Trantidis, Aris. 2015. "Is Contestability an Integral Part of the Definition of Democracy?" *Politics* 37(1): 67–81.

Trantidis, Aris. 2016a. *Clientelism and Economic Policy: Greece and the Crisis*. London: Routledge.

Trantidis, Aris. 2016b. "Clientelism and Economic Policy: Hybrid Characteristics and Collective Action in Greece." *Journal of European Public Policy* 23(10): 1460–1480.

Trantidis, Aris. 2017. "The Problem of Constitutional Legitimation: What the Debate on Electoral Quotas Tells Us about the Legitimacy of Decision-Making Rules in Constitutional Choice." *Constitutional Political Economy* 28(2): 195–208.

Trantidis, Aris 2022a. "Building an Authoritarian regime: Strategies for Autocratisation and Resistance in Belarus and Slovakia." *The British Journal of Politics and International Relations* 24(1): 113–135.

Trantidis, Aris. 2022b. "Progressive Constitutional Deliberation: Political Equality, Social Inequalities, and Democracy's Legitimacy Challenge." *Politics* 42(3): 453–469.

Trantidis, Aris. 2024a. "Government Externalities." *Public Choice* 201(3–4): 451–469.

Trantidis, Aris. 2024b. "State-Sponsored Capitalism and the Erosion of Liberal Democracy." In Juan Castaneda (ed.) *Government and Economic Growth in the 21st Century*. London: Routledge.

Trantidis, Aris, and Nick Cowen. 2024. "Is Public Ignorance a Problem? An Epistemic Defense of Really Existing Democracies." *Political Research Quarterly* 77 (3): 759–771.

Trantidis, Aris, and Vaso Tsagkroni. 2017. "Clientelism and Corruption: Institutional Adaptation of State Capture Strategies in View of Resource Scarcity in Greece." *British Journal of Politics and International Relations* 19(2): 263–281.

Trantidis, Aris, and Peter J. Boettke. 2022. "Macroeconomic Policy as an Epistemic Problem." *Journal of Public Finance and Public Choice* 37(2): 211–231.

Trantidis, Aris, and Nick Cowen. 2024. "Is Public Ignorance a Problem? An Epistemic Defense of Really Existing Democracies." *Political Research Quarterly* 77(3): 759–771.

Tufte, Edward R. 1978. *Political Control of the Economy*. Princeton, NJ: Princeton University Press.

Tullock, Gordon. 1967. The Welfare Costs of Tariffs, Monopolies, and Theft. *Western Economic Journal* 5(3): 224–232.

Tullock, Gordon. 2005. *The Rent-Seeking Society*. The Selected Works of Gordon Tullock, v. 5. Indianapolis, IN: Liberty Fund.

Van Bavel, Bas. 2016. *The Invisible Hand?: How Market Economies Have Emerged and Declined Since AD 500*. Oxford: Oxford University Press.

Van de Walle, Nicolas. 2007. "Meet the New Boss, Same as the Old Boss? The Evolution of Political Clientelism in Africa." In Hanspeter Kitschelt and Steven I. Wilkinson (eds.) *Patrons, Clients and Policies: Patterns of Democratic Accountability and Political Competition.* Cambridge: Cambridge University Press, pp. 50–67.

Wagner, Richard E. 2016. *Politics as a Peculiar Business: Insights from a Theory of Entangled Political Economy*. Cheltenham: Edward Elgar.

Wantchekon, Leonard. 2003. "Clientelism and Voting Behavior: Evidence from a Field Experiment in Benin." *World Politics* 55(3): 399–422.

Waterbury, John. 1992. "The Heart of the Matter? Public Enterprise and the Adjustment Process." In *The Politics of Economic Adjustment: International Constraints, Distributive Conflicts, and the State*, edited by Stephan Haggard and Robert R. Kaufman, 182–218. Princeton, NJ: Princeton University Press.

Weingrod, Alex. 1968. "Patrons, Patronage, and Political Parties." *Comparative Studies in Society and History* 10(4): 377–400.

Weitz-Shapiro, Rebecca. 2012. "What Wins Votes: Why Some Politicians Opt Out of Clientelism." *American Journal of Political Science* 56(3): 568–583.

Winters, Jeffrey A., and Benjamin I. Page. 2009. "Oligarchy in the United States?" *Perspectives on Politics* 7(4): 731–751.

Wittman, Donald. 1995. *The Myth of Democratic Failure: Why Political Institutions Are Efficient*. Chicago: University of Chicago Press.

Yıldırım, Kerem, and Herbert Kitschelt. 2020. "Analytical Perspectives on Varieties of Clientelism." *Democratization* 27(1): 20–43.

Cambridge Elements

Austrian Economics

Peter Boettke
George Mason University
Peter Boettke is a Professor of Economics & Philosophy at George Mason University, the BB&T Professor for the Study of Capitalism, and the director of the F. A. Hayek Program for Advanced Study in Philosophy, Politics and Economics at the Mercatus Center at George Mason University.

About the Series
This series will primarily be focused on contemporary developments in the Austrian School of Economics and its relevance to the methodological and analytical debates at the frontier of social science and humanities research, and the continuing relevance of the Austrian School of Economics for the practical affairs of public policy throughout the world.

Cambridge Elements

Austrian Economics

Elements in the Series

Austrian Capital Theory: A Modern Survey of the Essentials
Peter Lewin and Nicolas Cachanosky

Public Debt as a Form of Public Finance: Overcoming a Category Mistake and Its Vices
Richard E. Wagner

Defense, Peace, and War Economics
Christopher J. Coyne

Cultural Considerations within Austrian Economics
Virgil Storr and Arielle John

The Origins and Consequences of Property Rights: Austrian, Public Choice, and Institutional Economics Perspectives
Meina Cai, Llia Murtazashvili, Colin Harris and Jennifer Murtazashvili

The Political Economy of Public Pensions
Eileen Norcross and Daniel J. Smith

The Political Economy of Terrorism, Counterterrorism, and the War on Terror
Anne R. Bradley, Christopher J. Coyne and Abigail R. Hall

Understanding Ludwig Lachmann's Economics
Virgil Henry Storr and Solomon M. Stein

James Buchanan and Peaceful Cooperation: From Public Finance to a Theory of Collective Action
Alain Marciano

The Socialist Calculation Debate: Theory, History, and Contemporary Relevance
Peter Boettke, Rosolino A. Candela and Tegan L. Truitt

Institutional Diversity and the Economic Calculation Debate: The Feasibility Issue Revisited
Paul Dragos Aligica and Adrian Miroiu

Clientelism
Aris Trantidis

A full series listing is available at: www.cambridge.org/EAEC

For EU product safety concerns, contact us at Calle de José Abascal, 56–1°, 28003 Madrid, Spain or eugpsr@cambridge.org.

www.ingramcontent.com/pod-product-compliance
Lightning Source LLC
LaVergne TN
LVHW011850060526
838200LV00054B/4275